# Genius of Bath

*The city from Beacon Hill in 1848*

# Genius of Bath
## The City and its Landscape

## Christopher Pound

*To build, to plant whatever you intend,*
*To rear the Column, or the arch to bend,*
*To swell the terras, or to sink the Grot;*
*In all, let Nature never be forgot.*
*Consult the Genius of the Place in all...*

Alexander Pope
*An epistle to Lord Burlington, 1731*

## Millstream Books

*For Alistair, Graeme and Robyn*

I could not have prepared this book alone. Considerable help and encouragement have been given to me by my family and friends. In particular, I would like to thank Gill Clarke who has commented on several drafts and Peter Atkinson, David McLaughlin, Mary Stacey and Tim Graham who have all assisted with their comments. The staff at the Reference Library have all been very patient with requests and helpful in finding material. Jill Knight, the Keeper of Art at the Victoria Art Gallery, and Julie Brewer have also been most helpful in finding material. Finally, I am indebted to Pat Baynes who has patiently and cheerfully prepared the various drafts. To all of these I give my thanks.

Views which I have expressed in this book are my own and may not necessarily reflect those of my employer.

Illustrations are included by courtesy of:

David McLaughlin
Bath Reference Library
Victoria Art Gallery, Bath

First Published 1986

Millstream Books
7 Orange Grove
Bath
Avon BA1 1LP

This book is set in 12 point Bembo
Typeset by Addkey Print Ltd., Corsham
Printed in Great Britain by Netherwood Dalton & Co., Huddersfield

© Christopher Pound 1986

ISBN 0948975016

# Contents

*The city from Beechen Cliff in 1757 with Holloway and 'Paradise Row' in the foreground*

*...she voluntarily rejected the whole City of Bath as unworthy to make part of a landscape.*

> Jane Austen
> *Northanger Abbey*, 1818

# 1  An Unworthy City

A young man, Henry Tilney, persuaded a young lady to accompany him on a walk into the countryside outside Bath. The happy couple walked to the top of Beechen Cliff as countless numbers of couples have done over the years. On reaching the top of the cliff, Henry analysed the view and the landscape spread out below and around him. He talked of "...foregrounds, distances and second distances; side screens and perspectives; lights and shades..." His companion, Catherine, may have been disappointed in his choice of conversation, for she rejected the city below "as unworthy to make part of a landscape".

Jane Austen's account, from the beginning of the nineteenth century, raises two interesting points about Bath's present landscape and our attitudes to it. Firstly, it may be very unlikely that a young couple walking out today to the top of Beechen Cliff would analyse and criticise the landscape around them. Secondly, the landscape we would see today has changed considerably from that which Jane Austen enjoyed at the time of her brief stay in Bath. At the beginning of the nineteenth century she and her readers would have been familiar with the points that she has attributed to Henry Tilney in *Northanger Abbey*. Landscape was one of the arts discussed and practised by the gentry and the literati of the day. The picturesque landscape was a feature of popular Gothic novels by her contemporaries, whose interest in landscape extended from matters of aesthetics and taste to philosophy, reason and morality. "The same principles which direct taste in the polite arts," wrote Humphrey Repton in 1816, "direct judgement in morality". Jane Austen was impressed sufficiently by the work of Humphrey Repton to refer to him in her novel *Mansfield Park*. She was also described by her brother as a

*...warm and judicious admirer of landscape, both in nature and on canvas. At a very early age, she was enamoured of Gilpin on the Picturesque.*

Art and landscape were closely related, for the word 'picturesque' takes its name from a landscape which would create a 'picture'. Indeed the whole concept of a 'landscape' refers to an objective view of a scene and the very word is derived from the Dutch painter's word 'landskip' which is a representation of the countryside in a picture. At the end of the eighteenth century some of the more perceptive descriptions of Bath and its surrounding countryside came from writers such as Ibbetson, Laport and Hassell who were also artists.

> *An evening scene is productive of much more brilliant effect, the Crescents are then seen to the utmost advantage; their situation, their concave form, which catches a variety of light and their tone of colour are then peculiarly adapted to the pencil.* (5)

So wrote Ibbetson in 1793. Other writers described the countryside with references to the work of painters. Pierce Egan, describing Lansdown, wrote that

> *the scenery all around is bold as well as picturesque... The perspective is enchanting, and the local view likewise is interesting. Here and there a gentleman's seat is seen in the valley - the little spire of a country church - farmhouses and cottages - the fertile ground all around - the charming foliage of the trees - the extent of hedges dividing the various lands, the sheep feeding, etc. furnishing a most admirable landscape for the exquisite talents of a POUSSIN.* (6)

One of the difficulties of illustrating the early landscape by referring to contemporary literature as well as to drawings, is finding appropriate material. There is a wealth of eighteenth century material but as if to reflect the lack of concern for a picturesque view, or feel for landscape at the end of the nineteenth century, late Victorian novelists tended not to include descriptions of what they saw as their predecessors had done. Perhaps the age of the photograph was already replacing an age of good prose. There are, however, one or two notable exceptions. These include the novelist, William Black who, on a journey through Bath, described leaving Sydney Gardens on the canal and travelling up through the Avon valley on a wet spring day:

> *And then, by and by, when we had stolen through these closed and guarded paradises, behold! a great valley lay beneath us; and, beyond, a range of wooded heights with the suburbs of Bath stretching out, terrace on terrace into the open country. This Kennet and Avon Canal, winding snake like along the side of the hill, gave us wider and wider views as we glided onwards; the last traces of the City began to disappear; far below us the Avon gleamed, a thread of silver between its alders and willows, the heights arose into a series of receding woods along the horizon line... We felt as if we had come out of some cribbed and cabined place - a dark and depressing and liquid place - into a world of comfort and sweetness and pleasant sights and sounds. The gracious air about us was singing. We were glad to have done with the last of the towns.* (7)

William Black on looking back towards Grosvenor and Larkhall appears to show some relief on leaving the city for open countryside. For although Bath was still a small 'town' at the end of the eighteenth century, it was a relatively busy urban place.

Another Victorian novelist, Mary Mitford, visited Bath twice at the beginning of the Victorian era.

*A Victorian view from Beechen Cliff in 1854*

> *Bath is a very elegant and classical looking city. Standing upon a steep hillside, its regular white buildings rising terrace above terrace, crescent above crescent, glittering in the sun, and charmingly varied by the green trees of its park and gardens; its pretty suburban villas mingling with the beautiful villages that surround it on every side, nothing can exceed the grace and amenity of the picture... Very pleasant is Bath to look at.*

(8)

Mitford's visit was earlier than Black's boat trip and the buildings were still clean, but she was able to record the spread of the city which was also recorded on Cotterell's contemporary map of 1851. The Victorians were keen on walks or rambles away from the city and it is from books and articles describing these walks that we can glean descriptions of the countryside and the changing shape of Bath. An author of some of these accounts of rambles around Bath was Louise Wheatcroft, who wrote articles entitled 'Picturesque Village Rambles around Bath' in the *Bath Country Graphic* in 1897. She noted in these the development of the suburbs in Weston and Twerton. Earlier in 1819, Pierce Egan had described Twerton as a "neat and interesting looking village" but Mrs. Wheatcroft felt that "a village it can be styled no longer". Within a century Jane Austen's Bath had grown to absorb some of the surrounding villages.

(9)
10)

9

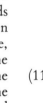

*Rocks and cascades in the grounds of 'Widcombe Manor', 1839*

At the beginning of the nineteenth century, Henry Tilney would have been able to see from Beechen Cliff a relatively small compact city with newer 'picturesque' development being constructed behind on the slopes of Lansdown and a number of new villas spreading up the Bathwick and Lyncombe Hills. The respective character of the various different periods of building in Bath can still be picked out from high points such as Beechen Cliff. R.A.L. Smith has observed of Bath: "we have epitomised, as it were, in microcosm the whole of the architectural history of England in the eighteenth century". This is also true of landscape history. Indeed the (11) history of urban landscape and landscaped gardens is inevitably tied to the suburban development of our cities. This relationship is easily understood when we examine eighteenth century and Regency development. Here terraces and villas were set in a garden landscape of a particular style, reflecting good taste; however, with one or two notable exceptions, there has not been in recent years the wish to create a particular style of landscape with new building. We are now reduced to regarding 'landscape' as the green space left over and around a new building rather than the context of the site which will contribute to and influence the design of the building.

Attitudes to our countryside and its landscape have clearly changed. Medieval man was suspicious of wild nature and with good reason, because men and beasts could make it dangerous. For them a good landscape was agricultural or a walled garden. Their attitude survived well into the seventeenth century for even John Evelyn showed some nervousness of 'hideous rocks' near Fontainebleau, the scene of "gloomy precipices, intermingled with trees and shrubs and monstrous protuberances of the huge stones which hang over and menace ruine..." After the eighteenth century landowners cultivated and dominated the English landscape, the same 'horrid rocks' and similar landscapes in the British Isles came to be regarded as 'picturesque' and appreciated as being sublime. Reference to contemporary literature not only gives us a clearer description of what many gardens and landscapes were like, but may help us to understand why our predecessors wished to create landscapes of a particular style.

The remnant of the eighteenth century landscape, today, is confused by the changes that have taken place. Trees planted before the eighteenth century have matured, died and been removed. Also later development has encroached into what may have been a planned or considered prospect. Enough of an early landscape survives in Bath for us to consider its conservation or management, but not for much longer if we achieve neither. To be effective in cherishing the city's landscape it is essential to understand how each part has been created. A better understanding involves an examination of the attitudes of our predecessors and our own. Whilst we can enjoy a mature landscape planted by Ralph Allen or perhaps Capability Brown we should remember that they could never have enjoyed their work as we can today. Will we ever understand what motivated our Georgian predecessors to plant for and cherish the city's landscape when we do not share their aesthetic values?

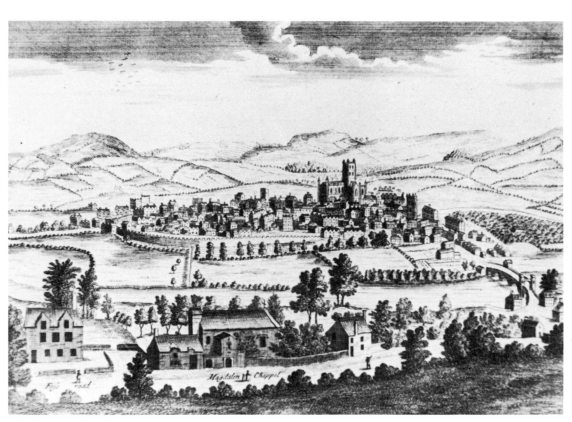

*Mead's view of Bath*
*from Beechen Cliff, 1723*

*Of the Bath before 1725 it is much more difficult to speak. Little remains above ground, and what remains refuses to form a picture.*

Nikolaus Pevsner
*Bristol and North Somerset,* 1958

# 2            A Pretty Place

As Pevsner found, it is difficult to imagine how early Bath looked from the buildings that remain. It is, however, easier with landscape because much of the countryside and woodland around the city that we can see today was formed in very early times, with the landscape assuming more of its present day appearance in the eighteenth century. One of the earliest true prints of Bath, dated 1723, shows a walled medieval city set in an agricultural landscape with some suburban ribbon development built along the main roads extending north to Walcot and south across the river. The countryside immediately adjacent to the city is all in use, as grazing land or market gardens. The hedgerows and trees are mature, suggesting that most of this land had been enclosed for some time. Those slopes that are too steep for farming are wooded.

Leland observed Bath from Holloway on Beechen Cliff in 1540:

> *...or ever I came to the bridge at Bath that is over Avon, I cam down by a rokky hille fulle fair of springes of water; and on this rokky hille is sette a longe streate as a suburbe of the Cyte of Bath and [in] this short streate is a chappelle of St. Mary Magdalen... The Cyte of Bath is sette booth yn a fruteful and pleasant bottom which is environed on every side with great hills, out of which cum many springes of pure water that be conveyed by dyverse wayes to serve the cite...*

Over a century later Celia Fiennes struggled around the country and came down the same road:

> *...down a very steep hill and stony a mile from the town scarce any passing and there descends a little current of water continually from the rocks; the wayes to the Bath are all difficult, the town lyes low in a bottom and its steep ascents all ways out of the town; ...the baths in my opinion makes the town unpleasant, the aire thicke and hot by their steem and by its own situation so low, encompassed with high hills and woods...*

Her enthusiasm for the city improved, however, by 1698 when she now called the city a "pretty place" and approached it from the other side of the valley where; "on Landsdon Summersetshire begins, which is a very

*Many early travellers recorded coming down Beechen Cliff which was once coppiced (Bucks' print, 1734)*

pleasant hill for to ride on for aire and prospect..." but she recorded also the (16) descent into Bath as a steep and stony narrow way.

The difficulties of these roads continued into the eighteenth century when they were compared by Ned Ward to the problems of travelling on the continent, where he was "persuaded the Alps are to be passed with less danger..." All early travellers such as Ward, Fiennes, Leland and Daniel (17) Defoe looked down from Holloway to see the view as recorded in the print by Richard Mead in 1723. A few years later the Buck brothers prepared their 1734 view of Bath, and like Mead, they showed countryside around the city. In their view we can see also the neighbouring villages of Weston and Twerton. The latter, then called Twiverton, is surrounded by what appears to be a significant area of woodland, of which only the present day

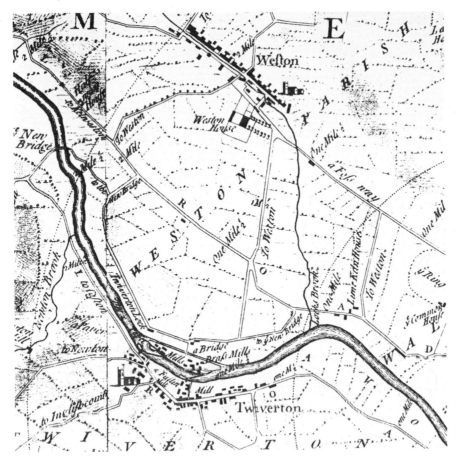

*Thorpe's map showed Weston and Twerton well outside the City in 1742*

Carr's Wood remains. Thorpe's map, prepared a few years later in 1742, shows these communities with a few buildings around their church but curiously does not show this woodland. These villages have now been absorbed into a larger Bath but they were then independent parishes and separated by countryside, poor roads and woods.

In the woods we can find remnants and forms of a much older countryside. Woodland had always played an important part in the early economy, providing timber for shipbuilding and material for fuel. After the destruction of the countryside that took place in the seventeenth century, a considerable amount of replanting followed throughout Britain. Much of this would have been on sites of earlier woodlands dating back to medieval hunting forests and even Saxon woods. The West Saxon King Ine had recognised the value of woodlands and found it necessary to protect them by legislation. Later Saxon charters make references to these woods and even individual trees as boundary markers. The Norman Domesday Book indicates relatively little woodland close to the city and of the few clues offered, the only area in Bath with a large amount of woodland was the Manor of Weston. Here the Locksbrook Stream, which used to run down Weston High Street, once marked the south-eastern limit of the great

8)
9)

15

medieval Kingswood Forest. This extended westwards from the brook as far as the River Severn and northwards from the River Avon as far as Alderly Brook in Gloucestershire. The Cotswold escarpment marked its eastern edge. This land was a Royal hunting forest and although the term 'forest' (20) was used for an area governed by the King's hunting laws, the area did contain many acres of woodland.

The distribution of early settlements, such as those identified in the Domesday Book, varied according to a number of factors, including cultural matters, although the most important were the quality of the soil and the availability of water. In the area around Roman Bath both of these were propitious so that the early villa estates and settlements have been found to be evenly spread around the valley, generally not more than a mile (21) apart. Archaeological investigations by Professor Finberg at Withington, near Chedworth in Gloucestershire, have shown that some present day parish boundaries come from the original Roman estate boundaries which survived through the Saxon period and were handed on virtually intact to (22) become church property. With the large number of villas that we know of around Roman Bath, it is very likely that some of the lines of present boundaries, roads and field patterns were established at that time.

There can be little doubt that a sizeable settlement at Bath survived the decline of the Roman age. The Saxon conquest of the Cotswold area culminated in the Battle of Dyrham in 577 AD. As a result of this victory, Saxons won the three 'cities' of Bath, Cirencester and Gloucester. Barry Cunliffe points out that the very mention of the towns at all is some indication that they were considered to be of importance, but what shreds of town life the Saxons inherited, he finds it is impossible to say. (23)

More evidence supports the thesis that Bath was a significant settled community, with the royal approval of Saxon charters which describe Bath as a 'burgh' having its own mint and later a growing Christian community in the monastery founded in 675 AD by Osric the Saxon, King of the Hurriccas. From this, Saxon Bath grew and prospered for another three hundred years until the city was razed to the ground in 1088 following the troubles associated with the death of William Rufus. The ruins might have been still warm when they were very soon bought by John de Villula and consecrated to the See of Somerset. Following this the construction of the Abbey was started.

With John de Villula's purchase, the land in and around the city remained church land from the time of the Domesday Book to the Dissolution of the Monasteries between 1536 and 1540. Then the land was sold off by the King's Commissioners. The extent of the church's ownership, which included great estates around Glastonbury, meant that this had a profound (24) effect on Somerset, more than on many other counties. The new owners enclosed most of this land on a piecemeal basis with various private agreements in the valleys, leaving areas for sheep grazing on the highest part of the Mendips. By the time John Leland went on his tour through England between 1534 and 1543, he noted that "...most part of al Somersetshire ys yn hegge row enclosid". He was observing a landscape soon after the (25) Dissolution and some of the hedgerows he saw may well have been earlier boundaries and field patterns which had survived from the Saxon estates.

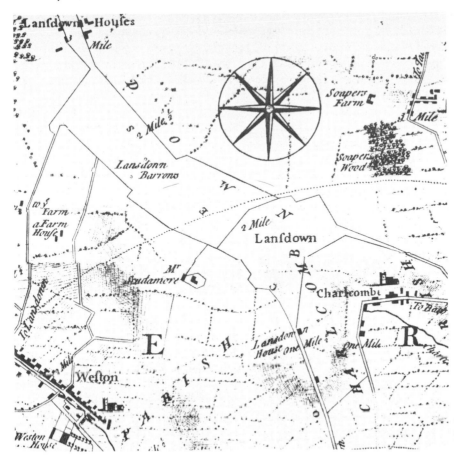

*Parts of Lansdown were shown not enclosed on Thorpe's map of 1742*

The importance of the clearly well-established wool trade to the towns in the Mendip area was very evident to John Leland. Of sixteenth century Bath, he noted that "...the town hath for a long time syns continually most maintained by making of clothe..." The Cotswolds and Mendips were then prospering from wool but sheep had been grazing on these limestone hills since Bronze Age times. On the tops of these hills a landscape has been created by sheep where vast flocks nibbled the rich vegetation, turning it into the characteristic springy turf over which we can walk today. The effects of the generations of grazing sheep on the hills around Bath were still much in evidence as late as the beginning of the nineteenth century. The *Bath Guide* of 1802 notes that

> *On Lansdown, famous for the number of sheep fattened by its delicate herbage, is annually held a very large fair on the 10th of August...*

Thorpe's map of 1742 shows that part of the tops of Lansdown and Claverton Down remained open and still not enclosed. Where enclosures were introduced later on the tops of these hills and elsewhere on the Mendips, they created what appears to be a 'planned landscape' with straight boundaries and roads.

17

Whilst Lansdown may still retain the delicate herbage described by the authors of the guide, it remains relatively treeless on the top as it would have been in the eighteenth century. However, on the other side of the valley on Claverton Down there are trees. In 1780 Edmund Rack, the founder of the Bath and West of England Society, noted that around Combe Down were extensive plantations of fir, which "throw a solemn gloominess of shade impervious to the sun and winds over a fine soft turve free from underwood..." The Rev. John Collinson describes in 1791 the ascent to the Down on the turnpike road as delightful, (28

> ...the upper part of the road being through a fine plantation of firs and forest trees on each side. The summit of the hill is adorned with wood, disposed in a manner that bespeaks the taste as well as the munificence of Mr. Allen; whole extensive and noble plantations are the pride and ornament of the surrounding country. (29)

Most of the eighteenth century travellers comment on these plantations of fir trees which have now been replaced by broad-leaved trees. In the middle of the eighteenth century Scots Pines and other firs had become fashionable, after the Duke of Cumberland's Culloden campaign in 1746. He, as Ranger of Windsor Great Park, later planted Scots Pines in clumps in the park. Collinson describes the top of the Claverton Down as (3

> ...having an exceeding fine turf, ornamented with clumps of firs and forest shrubs... on the north west brow, fronting the City, is a noble plantation of Scotch and spruce firs, containing many acres; in the foreground of which, and immediately under them, is the shell of a castle, erected by the late Mr. Allen. (31

Whether Ralph Allen planted his trees for effect, as a screen to his stone workings, or as a crop, we do not know, but Collinson notes that on Combe Down, Ralph Allen planted large groves of firs, commemorated now only in the name of a field, for the "laudable purposes of ornamenting" what was then a "rough and barren hill".

Ralph Allen was not the first to exploit the limestone available from the hills around Bath. The Romans had quarried for stone above both Bathampton Down and Bloomfield Road leaving there the 'gruffy' or disturbed ground at The Tumps. Since then, there was probably little stone working until after the eleventh century when the monastery and abbey were constructed. In the sixteenth century the quarries on Combe Down and Odd Down were observed by Leland, who, travelling from Midford, noted "...2 good miles al by montayne ground and quarre and little wood in syte". (32

Although most of the quarries on Combe Down and Hampton Down were largely worked out by 1810, they remained an 'industrial landscape', appreciated by the devotees of the Picturesque Movement who, in search of of a wild rugged landscape, found them a suitable subject for sketching. Collinson in his description of Monkton Combe in 1791, notes of the plateau above the village "...wild, but pleasing irregularities of the surface and the scenery, diversified with immense quarries". (3

The geological structure of the hills around Bath comprises layers of clay and limestone. Through this the river has cut a winding course, with steep hillsides and a micro-climate particularly suitable for growing vines. Thorpe's map shows a large area near Walcot marked as a vineyard. North of the London Road near to the present Snow Hill, there is still a 'Vineyard Cottage' and a street name, The Vineyards . These eighteenth century vineyards were claimed to produce reputable crops and wines. John Aubrey considered the vineyards at Claverton, planted in his day by Sir William Bassett, to be the best in England. Wine was still being made from the Claverton grapes in 1705.

34)

On the clay and limestone slopes, oak and ash trees grew as the natural species and remained dominant until the eighteenth century when beech trees were introduced by a variety of landlords. However, Ralph Allen planted firs on his estate. His Clerk of Works, Richard Jones, notes in his autobiography that in 1742 he began to plant a former rabbit warren on Bathampton Down.

*The first portion planted is now called Fir Forest and then he began to plant firs all over his estate... Never was a so great a plantation [planted] by one private gentleman, in all 55,146.*

35)

John Britton noted that by 1830

*Open stone quarries above Bath drawn by Hassell in 1798*

*Harrison's walks shown on the Bucks' print, 1734*

to the East, South and North of Bath are the steep hills of Claverton, Beechen Cliff, Lansdown, the slopes of which are clad with a variety of Pine and other trees.

(36)

Some of these woods were shown a century earlier in the Buck brothers' print of 1734. They took their prospect from Widcombe Hill and their print shows the new 'Palladian' style development of Queen Square, Trim Street and Green Street emerging from the medieval city. They may have indulged in some exaggeration, because the new buildings appear to rise dramatically over the smaller, earlier buildings. Exaggerated or not, the character of the city was now changing and dominated by the Georgian development. One development recorded on the print is Harrison's Assembly Rooms. These with their gardens and tree-lined walks along the river were described by Mary Chandler at the time:

Round the green walk the River Glides away,
Where midst Espaliers balmy Zephyrs play.

(37)

The earlier maps of seventeenth century Bath show very few 'public' open spaces within the walls. There are a few garden walks and bowling greens and these appear to be the only spaces available for recreation. This was also the situation when Celia Fiennes made her earlier visits to the city. She must have recovered from her difficult descent by the time she reached the city because here she found everything to be pleasant:

20

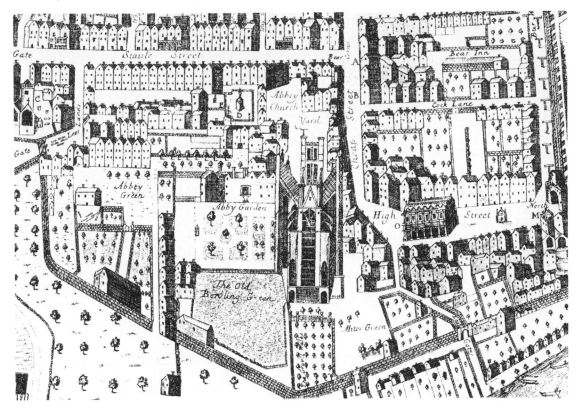

*I now proceed to describe the rest of the town; there are green walkes very pleasant and in many places, and out of the Cathedrall you walk in to the Priory which has good walkes of rows of trees which is pleasant; there are deans, prebends and doctors houses which stand in that green, which is pleasant, by the Church called the Abby which is lofty and spacious, and much Company walke there especially in wet weather... in that Kings Mead there are severall little Cake-houses where you have fruit Sulibubs and sumer liquours to entertaine the Company that walke there.*

38)

39)

Shortly after Celia Fiennes' visit, Joseph Gilmore prepared his celebrated map of Bath in about 1692. The pleasant walks which she had referred to are shown near the Abbey and these were to develop into the eighteenth century parades. The Abbey Green survives but not the bowling green, alongside which Gilmore and earlier cartographers show a typical Stuart garden layout with a quincunx, or a formal pattern of five trees, one of which is in the centre. This suggests a remnant of earlier gardening practice and perhaps the formal patterns of the medieval knot gardens which had survived the demise of the priory. Keith Thomas suggests the early gardens had a spiritual dimension, related to the conception of paradise, for in the later middle ages, 'Paradise' had been the term for the pleasure garden of a monastery or convent. These early priory gardens may survive today only in the name of the buildings next to John de Villula's church in the Holloway. Here was Paradise Row and now only Paradise Hotel.

*Gardens of Ladymead House in the 17th century*

Ladymead House and gardens as depicted in the early 18th century oil painting showing the c1680 house

The best picture of an early urban garden in Bath is in a painting of Ladymead House. Whilst this property is outside the city walls and the original building has changed considerably, the structure of the original garden survives. The painting, which dates from the 1680s, shows a walled garden sloping down to the river. The garden is laid out in a very simple but formal style of symmetrical patterns of paths and parterres which were fashionable at that time. Alongside the garden is a straight canal which marks the parish boundary. This and other similar gardens, as well as

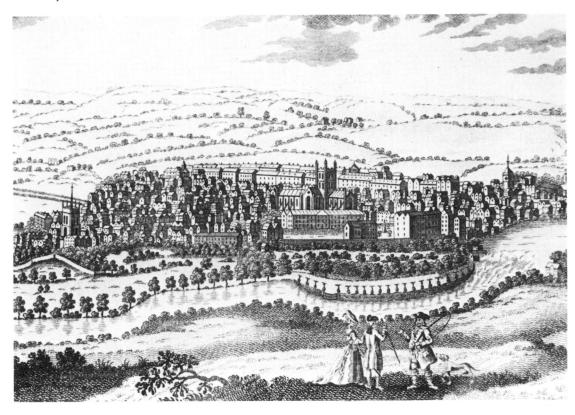

providing an area of privacy and recreation, would also have provided some of the fruit and vegetables for the household. Here in Walcot, the suburban houses were more fortunate than houses within the city walls, where the size of the garden was very much smaller, offering little relief from the squalor of the city.

*In the middle of the 18th century Bath was still a small city*

By the middle of the eighteenth century, the suburban development of the city has not yet really encroached into the countryside. Dr. Richard Pococke on his travels through England in 1754, could still write:

(40)

> *Bath is situated in a narrow valley between high hills. The present town, with a few gardens and meadows to the south and west have the river on three sides. The old town is encompassed with walls except in about an eighth part of it on the river to the east...*

The end of the seventeenth century, however, marks the beginning of a process which changed this 'medieval' city and its surroundings and also the beginnings of a change in attitudes to the landscape.

*Widcombe Church with Prior Park mansion in the background (1786 print)*

*The taste refin'd appeals in yonder Wood*
*Not nature tortured, but by Art improv'd*

Mary Chandler
*The Description of Bath*, 1735

# 3      A Palladian House

Thorpe's 1742 map shows Walcot as a village just about separate from the city walls. It was, however, essentially a suburb, providing a more pleasant environment but still close to the city. The villages of Weston and Twerton were too far away to be considered as suburbs during the eighteenth century. Widcombe and Lyncombe, however, were very close but remained one independent parish until 1835. In these suburbs lay an opportunity for houses for people who did not wish to or could not live in the city. In Lyncombe, and in particular Holloway, people who wished to escape the jurisdiction of the law enforcement in the city could settle below Beechen Cliff and still be close to the city. Others who wished to live away from the city could find more respectable accommodation in the old village of Widcombe.

The ownership by the church of much of the land around the city, may be the reason that no large family estates were established and with them no 'traditional' family manor houses. Widcombe Manor is the nearest we have to such a manor house standing in its own grounds close to the church and village. An earlier house may have been on this site before the present building was built in 1727 for Philip Bennet who eventually became a Member of Parliament for Bath. Here the medieval and tudor tradition of walled gardens continues, protecting an air of respectable gentility. These grounds can be glimpsed through the iron-work gates near to the church of St. Thomas à Becket.

Whilst the Manor house may have been one of the earliest important buildings in the village it is now dominated by the mansion of Prior Park. This later building at the top of the valley above Widcombe asserts itself by its scale, setting and grandeur. Prior Park is of special importance because it is both a fine example of a large country house in early eighteenth century Palladian style and, just as important, an example of grounds which were laid out just when fashion and attitudes to landscape design were changing. The house and gardens hosted visits by literary and political figures of the day, who discussed and wrote about landscape and in various ways influenced the landscape of both the city and the estate itself. Of these, Alexander Pope was the most influential. He had not only determined taste in architectural and landscape matters on estates throughout the country, but contributed to the gardens of Prior Park as a friend of the owner. The owner of the mansion and the man who caused it to be built was Ralph Allen, a self-made man whose fortune was based on his success in re-organising the postal system. It enabled him to acquire, in 1726, extensive rights to stone workings in Combe Down in the hills above Bath. Allen had used some considerable ingenuity to improve the marketing of his stone products in order to reach a wider market at a lower cost, with innovations such as a windlass system and, in 1731, a 'railway' which took stone from his mines and quarries down to the river. Allen had earlier been an investor in the construction of the Twerton 'Cut', a short length of canal, which contributed to making the river navigable for traffic from Bristol.

Chance favoured the prepared man, because Allen's successful development of his stone quarries coincided with the city becoming increasingly attractive as a resort and with its early Georgian expansion. Architects such as John Wood and John Strahan were by now preparing various schemes for new building outside the city walls. This early success of the city was, however, no accident and was due to Richard 'Beau' Nash. His influential role as Master of Ceremonies had created Bath as a safe, ordered and fashionable place, suitable for and attractive to society from London and elsewhere. The rules he introduced not only established a climate and economy stable enough to attract customers, but attracted investment to the city. This investment financed development which used stone from Allen's quarries. Following a failure to secure the contract for the building of Greenwich hospital and to show the world in general what his stone could do, a spot was chosen for a new house on his estate which according to Ibbetson "...having been an appendage to the priory still retained its romantic name". Allen bought the land which had been parkland and part (4: of the former Priory Deer Park. Leland had noted in his itinerary:

> *A mile at this syde Bathe by south east, I saw 2 parks enclosed with a ruinous stone wall now withe out dere. One longyd to byshoppe and the other to the Prior of Bath...* (4:

The monks had created a fine park for the Prior's country seat. The Prior did not, however, choose to live on the top of the hill but his house may have been further down the slope where the present fishponds are. William Tyte (4- states that the park was well stocked with deer, and Austin King refers to "vineyards and gardens and shady groves, and wide stretches of pasturage". (45 Here Allen was able to find a site for his new mansion with magnificent natural views down the valley across the village of Widcombe and to the city. We should remember that at this time Bath had not grown eastwards and so Allen would have looked across to the countryside and woodland as shown on the Buck brothers' print. The architect, John Wood, was commissioned to prepare drawings for the building. In copying the early designs for a mansion at Wanstead, Wood had to find the right contour, but by siting the building to take advantage of these views, the contours largely determined the curve in its plan.

Successful entrepreneurs of the seventeenth and eighteenth centuries such as Ralph Allen differed from the established landed gentry. They had

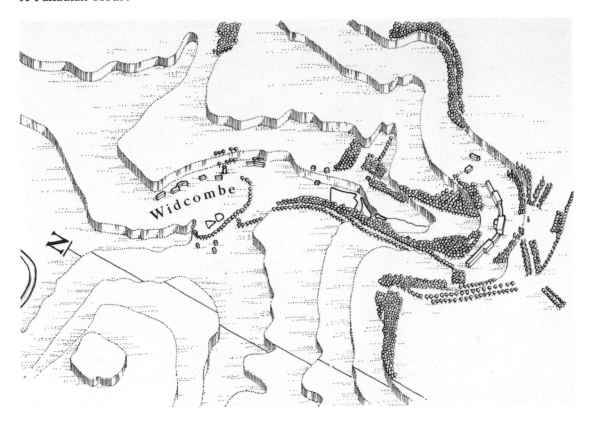

Widcombe

N

made their fortunes from commerce or investments, such as in coal or minerals, and not from an existing agricultural estate or the development of their urban property. In most cases, these nouveaux riches were Whigs and did not come from the established Tory gentry with a traditional manor house on a country estate. They were therefore able to construct new mansions such as Prior Park or the Blathwayts' earlier mansion at Dyrham, free from the ties of a traditional estate and in the current or fashionable architectural style. The eighteenth century gentleman building a new Palladian mansion in fashionable grounds had either to create a new landscape, with the necessary views across the countryside, or radically alter other existing buildings. Contemporary accounts note that Allen did not cut down the mature trees to model his new landscape. Mary Chandler in her 1735 poem *The Description of Bath* describes the beginning of the work at Prior Park:

*Prior Park in its topographical context (based on a map of c.1750)*

46)

47)
48)

> On this fair Eminence the Fabric stands
> The finish'd Labour of a thousand Hands;
> The Hill, the Dale, the River, Groves and Fields
> Vary the Landscape which thy Prospect yields...
> ...Thy taste refin'd appears in yonder Wood,
> Not Nature tortured, but by Art improv'd:
> Where cover'd Walks with open Vistas meet,
> An area here, and there a shady seat.

49)

27

*Visitors enjoying Prior Park and its grounds*

By 1734 Wood had completed some buildings in the centre of the city and had mastered the rules of Palladian architecture. He was well-read in classical literature, history and the architectural publications of the day. He would have been familiar with the three volumes of Colin Campbell's *Vitruvius Britannicus* which had all been published in 1725, and also Campbell's various designs for a mansion at Wanstead, on which Prior Park is based. Allen's original building consisted of a central mansion with pavilions on either side, linked by loggias. Although Allen's Clerk of Works, Richard Jones, effected some amendments to the original design and later owners made further changes, the form of the mansion is essentially that conceived by John Wood.

The house was completed in 1741, ready to be lived in by Ralph Allen. Two years earlier the poet, Alexander Pope, had visited Bath and Allen's new house. In due course, he was to befriend Allen and for a while influenced the layout of the grounds. At about the time Allen moved into the house, Thorpe surveyed the property and published his map. This very detailed map of Bath shows the estate and clearly indicates the original layout of the grounds. However, with the help of Pope and others, the designs for the grounds were to change to reflect current gardening fashions. Allen kept an open house, using it as a 'show house', an advertisement for the products of his stone quarries. The mansion and the grounds included many more stone details, particularly in the interiors of the buildings, than we might expect in similar buildings. The grounds were (50 laid out with stone ornaments, steps and balustrades to be admired by the (51 many visitors, and no doubt Allen hoped they would emulate him and buy his stone to do it. The grounds and setting of the mansion not only made the best of a magnificent site, but they were laid out in a way that was clearly intended to impress. Impressive they are and it is likely that they influenced the design of gardens elsewhere.

*The fishponds in the Prior Park estate in 1834*

Many of the visitors to Prior Park wrote about the house and grounds. Among these visitors were politicians, artists and writers who included William Pitt, Henry Fielding and Samuel Richardson. Many of them described the gardens in their letters and novels. One visitor to Prior Park would have been the poet, William Shenstone, a close friend of the Rev. Richard Graves, the Rector of nearby Claverton. Through this friendship, and on one of his visits to Graves, Shenstone learnt of new landscape theory and early 'ferme ornée' gardens then being laid out by Philip Southcot at Woburn Farm in Surrey. Shenstone was sufficiently impressed by these gardens to lay out a new garden landscape on his own property at Leasowes in Shropshire and is now perhaps better known for his famous garden than for his poetry. He and Pope were both important as publicists for the new fashion of Landscape Gardening.

English landscape gardening in the eighteenth century can be placed into three or four periods, each associated with an identifiable style or approach to garden design. At the beginning of the century, the established fashion was a formal style whose antique geometry reflected the earlier Stuart landscape practice brought to England by the court of Charles II after the Restoration. The combination of Le Nôtre's French style of gardening and Dutch landscape work created formal gardens with straight lines, walks and rides similar to those which can still be seen at Versailles and in prints of early English gardens such as Dyrham. Then, in the first decades of the eighteenth century, ideas emerging from the 'Enlightenment' centred around the concept of simplicity and uniformity in Nature. Pope and his friends advocated a new philosophy of garden landscape design which avoided the straight lines of the then current landscape philosophy to create a natural landscape where "all art consists in the imitation and study of Nature". This style developed in due course with the work of Lancelot

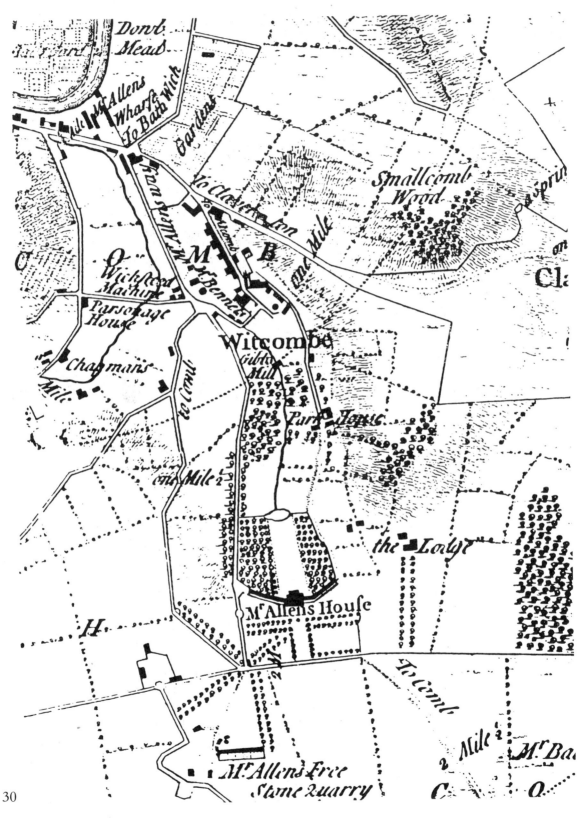

Donb.
Mead

Mr Allens
Wharfe
To Bath Wick

Gardens

Smallcomb
Wood

To Claverton Ann

one Mile

Cla

O
Wichstead
Machine

M

B

Mr Bennett

Parsonage
House

Witcombe

Gibbs
Mill

Chapman's

Mile

To Comb

Park House

one Mile 2

the Lodge

Mr Allens House

H

To Comb

2 Mile 2

Mr Ba

C

O

Mr Allens Free
Stone Quarry

*Note the formal treelined*
*rides shown on Thorpe's*
*map of the estate in*
*1742*

'Capability' Brown to become a contrived 'natural' countryside with long views to lakes framed by woods. At the end of the century, perhaps as a reaction to this inoffensive landscape, a more picturesque and dramatic style of Gothic Revival architecture and landscape evolved. That Allen was influenced by the new fashions, there can be no doubt. Thorpe's map, surveyed at about the time Allen first went to live in the mansion, shows the land close to the mansion planted with trees in straight lines. A 'rond-point' of tree-lined walks or rides radiating away from the mansion is clearly shown on Thorpe's map. The lines of these remain in the alignment of some roads in Combe Down. A change to the new landscape can be seen very clearly in Walker's interesting engraving of Prior Park Mansion at about 1750. This print shows the north side of the mansion before the stairs and present lower road were built in front of the portico and shows Allen's railway with trucks taking stone from his quarries down to his riverside wharf in Widcombe. In the background, perhaps in a representational form, are a line of fir trees. By planting these firs, Allen transformed a windswept sheep pasture. Samuel Derrick, a Master of Ceremonies in the city, in a letter of 1763 records that the ground about the mansion is

*Walker's print shows formal hedges and some informal tree planting c.1750*

> *charmingly disposed and improved, the gardens watered and laid out in taste, and Mr. Allen has planted a vast number of firs in the neighbourhood which thrive well. The ride bordering the grounds is miles in extent in which the views of the city, river and adjacent country are*

*Hearne's drawing records
a more mature informal
landscape in 1784*

*every minute so varied, that to me it wears the appearance of fairy ground;
nothing can be more enchanting.*

(5.

On the eastern side of the mansion is a formal garden behind a straight hedge. By contrast, the land behind the wall and immediately adjacent to the 'railway' has been laid out with a serpentine path winding through an informal layout of what appears to be fairly well-established trees. This path and informal design is not shown in Thorpe's map of eight years earlier, which clearly shows an older approach framing the view with plantations laid out with straight edges. Mary Chandler also reflected an earlier approach of planting with borders:

*A thousand sweets in mingled Odours flow
From blooming Flower's which on the Borders grow*

(5.

In the informal grove of trees are the remains of a grotto built by Allen and a sham bridge in the form of a sunken temple creating a pool. This was designed by Pope who also prepared in 1741 an inscription for a statue of Moses. Features such as these and a serpentine walk had also been included in Pope's earlier garden at Twickenham, to which Ralph Allen had sent stones for the grotto. How much Pope's interest touched on interference is difficult to say, but he shared with Ralph Allen an interest in horticulture. John Searle, Pope's gardener, was despatched from Twickenham to Bath to

(5.

*A wood engraving of the gothic temple*

assist with the laying out of the greenhouses and certainly Pope influenced the gardens at Prior Park from the beginning. Since there was no tradition of a former estate, the tree planting in Thorpe's map and formal gardens in Walker's print reflected earlier gardening practice at the time of the construction of the mansion, later abandoned, or adjusted, in favour of Pope's more natural layout.

This new landscape was associated also with philosophical sentiments and political aspirations, particularly those of 'liberty'. Pope, Shenstone, and others related their serpentine walks, groves and grottoes to themes from classical literature. However, not all the inspiration for gardens came from literature; many young gentlemen went on the Grand Tour to classical Europe and returned with ideas, loot and souvenirs which include paintings of classical scenes by Claude, Salvator Rosa or Poussin. Pope declared in 1734 "all gardening is landscape painting... just like a landscape hung up". Whilst neither Allen nor John Wood went on the Grand Tour, they were well-read and like others who did not go overseas, will have admired imported paintings which showed grottoes and temples as important elements in classical landscape.

In due course, small buildings and other features were added to the Prior Park estate including a temple and a bridge, introduced either as eye-catchers, or as places for the owner and his guests to pause and reflect. In spite of Allen's friend, Horace Walpole, not approving gothic summer houses, a 'gothic' temple was built by Richard Jones, Allen's Clerk of

33

Works, in 1745.  It survives, relocated in 1921 to the nearby Rainbow Wood House.  A gardener's house was also built in a gothic style to a design by Jones. The most celebrated addition to the landscape is the Palladian Bridge probably built by Jones in 1755.  This bridge is a copy of the 1737 Palladian bridge at Wilton and similar to another existing copy at Stowe and two others since gone.  It provides "the realisation of a project of Palladio that he never executed", writes Sacheverell Sitwell, "an architectural problem... the solution is so ideal that it has become mysterious".  This surrealist structure complements the 'arcadian landscape' by providing an appropriate focus and an illusion of greater distance in the middle foreground of the view from the mansion, just as a painter, such as Claude, would have created a similar arcadian landscape on canvas.

The new landscapes were not only described in paintings; Pope and Shenstone also set out their new landscape ideas in poems and essays. Allen's friend, Henry Fielding, who was reputed to dine at Prior Park every day, based his character Squire Allworthy on Allen, in his novel, *Tom Jones.* In this novel he alludes to the grounds, but a more positive description is provided by Samuel Richardson.  He was a sometime editor of Daniel Defoe's *A Tour through the whole Island of Great Britain* and in his 1742 edition of this he included a description of the estate.  This was in spite of the fact that Defoe had visited Bath over seventy years earlier and had died ten years before Allen built his mansion.  Richardson provided a still more extensive account of a gentleman's estate in his 1753 novel, *The History of Sir Charles Grandison.*  This description can only be based on Prior Park for it includes the various parts of the grounds, the stream and cascades, and refers to the planting outside the grounds of "...three rows of trees...one of pines; one of cedars; one of Scotch firs, in the like semi circular order".  This is the first account of Rainbow Wood, named on account of its shape.

Richardson declares that "the park is remarkable for its prospects, lawns and rich appearing clumps of trees of large growth".  His contemporaries confirm Mary Chandler's earlier lines "Not Nature tortured, but by Art improv'd", and the presence of large and mature trees. In May 1754, the *Universal Magazine* noted that Allen had "levelled no hills, but enjoys the beauty of the prospects they afford;  he has cut down no woods but stuck through them fine walks, and has, by that means, a delightful grove always filled with birds".  Another visitor, Dr. Richard Pococke, says at the same time that the gardens were laid out in "a wilderness".  Perhaps with Pope's influence the grounds were taking on the natural form that Richardson described in 1753, a landscape similar to 'studied naturalism' devised by Capability Brown but with mature trees already in place.

Tradition claims that Capability Brown contributed to the design of the Prior Park grounds and caused the bridge to be built, but apart from possibly influencing the layout in the late 1750s, we know of no major commission here.  His first known commissions in the West Country were after the construction of the bridge, at Longleat in 1757, Corsham 1760 and Newton Park in 1761.  He then completed designs for Bowood in 1763 and four years later at Kelston for a house designed by John Wood's son.

It is very probable that Brown would have stayed in Bath on one, or all, of these occasions and certainly would have visited Prior Park.  After Allen's death in 1764, his executors paid a sum of £60.0.0. to "Lancelot Brown esquire a debt owing from the testator Ralph Allen to him for surveying and making plans at or about Prior Park for him at his request". When he undertook this is not known, but Bryan Little suggests that it was probably in 1762. There is, however, an earlier *Plan of an Estate belonging to Ralph Allen, Eqr.* drawn up by Thomas Thorp (sic) and a man called Overton in about 1741. For £60 it is unlikely that Brown would have undertaken much or any design or supervision work, because the fee for such work at Kelston Park was considerably larger, at £500.

The inventory of Ralph Allen's estate listed all of the items not disposed of in his will. It included domestic items from the kitchen and garden shed and also some five dozen deer. More significant is the list of trees in the Prior Park grounds and outlying parts of the estate such as on Horsecombe. Apart from the many fruit trees, including oranges, at the time of his death Allen had planted nearly ten thousand trees. Some of these or their progeny remain on the Prior Park estate with the remnants of Pope's gardens and, of course, the fishponds and Palladian Bridge. From the contemporary descriptions it is clear that Allen had been able to enjoy in his deer park a landscape which included mature trees surviving perhaps from the medieval deer park.

Rudolf Wittkower has described a paradox concerning the large houses built in the seventeenth and early eighteenth centuries. The late seventeenth century baroque houses were becoming ornate but with geometric and formal gardens. The later Palladian houses were an austere and disciplined architecture but were surrounded in due course by informal English landscaped grounds. What is particularly interesting at Prior Park is that the estate included both a formal garden approach and latterly an informal landscape. This landscape retained the mature trees from earlier times and was perhaps enjoyed in this way by Capability Brown himself. We can enjoy it today because the estate has a very special relationship with the city, forming a background to the historic centre. There can be very few mansions with extensive grounds surviving to be surrounded by a growing city.

*Queen Square, the 'Palladian' masterpiece of the city (Cozens' print, 1773)*

*As one who long in populous city pent*
*Where houses thick and sewers annoy the air*
*Forth issuing on a summer's morn to breathe*
*Among the pleasant villages and farms*
*Adjoined from each thing met conceives delight*
*The smell of grain, or tedded grass, or kine,*
*Or dairy, each rural sight, each rural sound.*

John Milton
*Paradise Lost*, 1667

# 4     The Palladian City

(70)

Milton's seventeenth century London appears to have been unpleasant and eighteenth century Bath offered little improvement. In his *Description of Bath* John Wood deplored the foulness of the streets where there were "offensive gutters running above ground" into which "night soil, horse dung and slaughter house offal might be tipped". The attractions of the surrounding countryside were obvious. As well as Ralph Allen's estate there were now various recreation grounds or pleasure gardens around the city.

71)

Two of these are shown on Thorpe's map of 1742 not far from Prior Park. One of them, 'Lyncombe Spaw', was an earlier lodging for Mary Beatrice of Modena, the Consort of James II, who in 1687 stayed for a while in Bath. With a lack of proper accommodation in the city offering the right privacy and security in those troublesome times, she stayed with her court at a house in Lyncombe. The Paragon School occupies the site in a later building but in the 1730s the grounds were developed as a pleasure garden around a spa. Sydney Sydenham notes that the spring may have been known as early as the seventeenth century but it was rediscovered by a Mr. Milsom in 1737. In the same year, John Wood designed a circular building for 'Lyncombe Spaw'. Shortly after this the spring practically disappeared but was still shown on Thorpe's Map. In the 1750s the pleasure garden was revived which as a well known local resort called either Lyncombe Spaw or St. James's Palace, survived to the end of the eighteenth century. Thorpe shows a second rival and neighbouring resort on the site of the present Welton Lodge, less celebrated perhaps, except for its wonderful name of 'Wicksteed's Machine'.

72)

By the middle of the eighteenth century the city extended not much further than the grounds of Ralph Allen's Prior Park. The city had begun to grow shortly before Prior Park was built, with the early development of Green Street and Trim Street and later John Strahan's development of Kingsmead Square and Beaufort Square in 1725. These were just outside the city walls which had hitherto kept the city fairly compact apart from Walcot and Holloway. We have seen from Celia Fiennes' accounts, as well as from early maps and prints, that there were very few public open spaces. The new development within the city was providing new attractions and assembly rooms as well as providing accommodation. John Wood shows Harrison's Rooms and walks on his plan of 1735. Mary

*Orange Grove was originally laid out with rows of trees (from a fan of 1737)*

Chandler observes in the same year that some of the few open spaces were now being developed.

> *Where the smooth Bowl was wont to skim the Green*
> *Now Stately Rooms for Pleasure change the Scene.*

(73)

To some extent the hard urban character of the centre of the city remains to this day. Only Orange Grove and the last remains of the Priory Gardens at Abbey Green survive from early open spaces. North of the Abbey, the street pattern within the walls retains the lines of the Saxon 'burgh' described by John Evelyn in 1654 as narrow, uneven and unpleasant. Nearby, the wider High Street was the site of the market and an earlier Guildhall building. The Sawclose had always remained free from

(74)

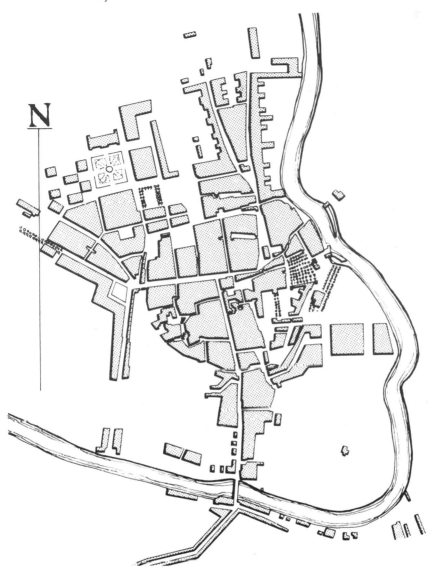

N

*Extent of the city in the 1740s (based on Thorpe's map)*

development but the present open spaces around the Abbey have been opened up relatively recently.

The new developments in the city, however, introduced new open spaces. Apart from two early schemes by John Strahan, the most important by far are those created by John Wood and his son. Strahan created streets of relatively modest terraced houses stretching away from small squares. Beaufort Square still provides a green space and focus for the surrounding houses. This is earlier than the theatre and there is no evidence that Strahan intended to provide anything more than this subtle space. Kingsmead Square is now dominated by a large plane tree surrounded by a hard surface of stone setts, but a plan of 1776 shows the square laid out with a formal garden similar to John Wood's Queen Square.

39

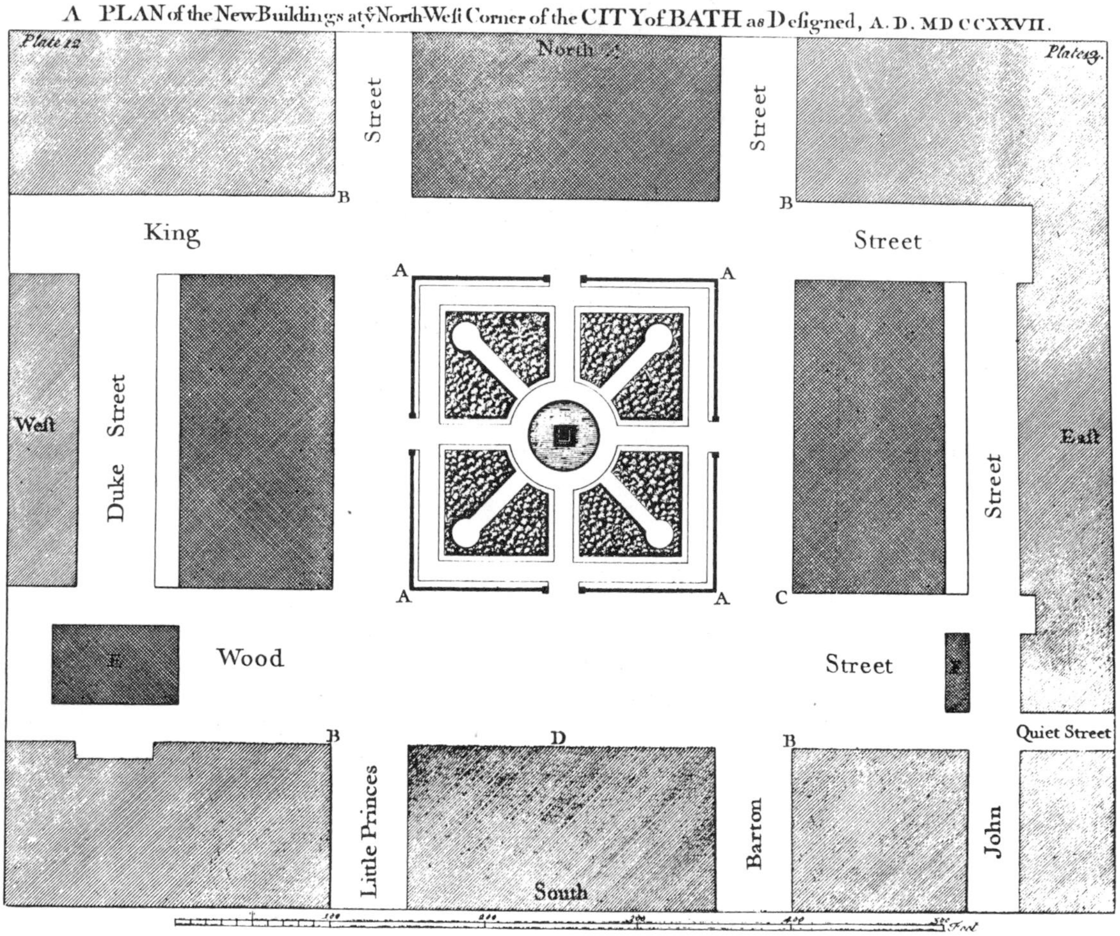
A PLAN of the New Buildings at ye North West Corner of the CITY of BATH as Designed, A. D. MDCCXXVII.
Plate 12
North
Street
Street
Plate 13
B
B
King
Street
A
A
West
Duke Street
East
Street
A
A
C
Wood
Street
Quiet Street
B
D
B
Little Princes
Barton
John
South
Feet

*Wood's plan for Queen Square shows a formal garden in the centre*

In 1728 John Wood began work on this, his most ambitious venture so far. The square took eight years to build and was not completed in its present form until the west side was filled in by the younger John Pinch in 1830. Originally this side had been the site of a central mansion set back from the pavement and flanked by symmetrically treated groups of houses. This first major urban development on the edge of the city is important both in terms of Bath's historical development and also for English architectural development. Wood's skill here was to create 'urban' palaces in the Palladian style on three sides of the square. The scale of each suited a nobleman but provided within each 'palace' an individual house linked by one grand facade and available to people of more modest means. Robert Southey described in 1807 "a square of which the sides resemble so many palaces". The attractions of this arrangement were obvious and its success (75
immediate because it was soon to be copied elsewhere both in the city and throughout England.

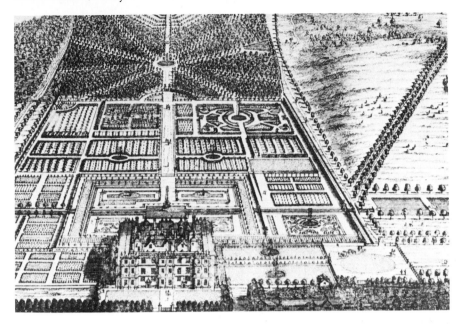

*The 17th century parterres shown on a print of Longleat, 1725*

Unlike Beaufort Square, which is really just an open space, the area in the centre of Queen Square was a formal garden, deliberately designed to complement the buildings around its edge. John Wood was most definitely interested in garden design. His account of Queen Square in the *Description of Bath* includes the garden space within the square in some detail and it is described before the elevations of the surrounding buildings. This suggests that he regarded the garden to be of prime importance. We should remember that when the Square was built it was a suburban development with no traffic passing through and so the garden would have been a haven of peace and a suitable place in which to perambulate or relax. The original effect was to recreate the parterre of the classical garden in front of a seventeenth century mansion. Such a parterre had been laid out at Longleat in about 1700. Compare the geometric design in the further parterre on the right with the design drawn by Wood for the layout within Queen Square.

Wood's description of the Square indicates that he had originally intended to have the site of the garden square levelled. This would have been in keeping with the formal Palladian composition of the north and south sides. Lack of funds prevented him from implementing his original intention. However, he also states that the costs of laying out the square in the form of a garden were greater than if it had just been paved. The gardens were laid out originally as gravelled walks, with a pool in the centre from which rose the obelisk.

> ...*I preferred an inclosed Square to an open one, to make this as useful as possible: For the Intention of a Square in a City is for People to assemble together; and the Spot whereon they meet, ought to be separated from the Ground common to Men and Beasts, and even to Mankind in General, if Decency and good Order are necessary to be observed in such Places of Assembly; of which, I think, there can be no doubt.*

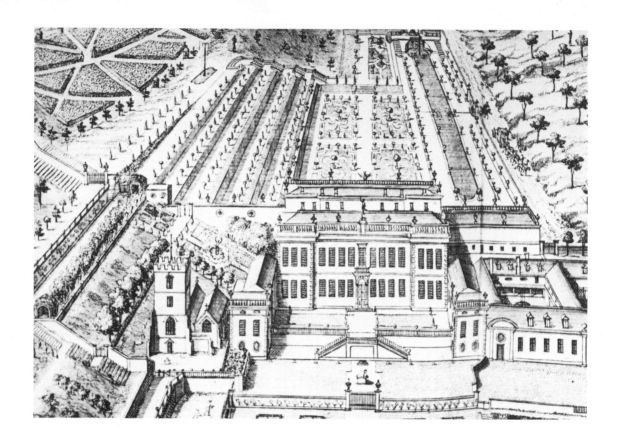

*Paths in the 'wilderness' above and behind the mansion at Dyrham (Kip's print)*

In spite of his preference for an 'inclosed square', Wood's next major development was North and South Parades and Duke Street. Here the opportunity for people to assemble is on the parade, a paved area outside the square of terraces. This was intended to be part of a more extensive development planned as a 'Roman Forum'. It was originally built with Grand Parade and Pierrepont Street as pedestrian streets but only Duke Street survives as such to this day.

In the *Description of Bath* Wood includes a print of 'St. James Triangle' in what is now Parade Gardens with a formal layout similar to some of the patterns which can be seen in seventeenth century parterres. John Wood probably would have been familiar with such gardens at Dyrham. It is now an accepted fact that he may have been born in, or near, Bath, possibly in the Swainswick area, where there is evidence of earlier generations of a family called Wood. His birth in 1704 would have made him eight years old when Kip drew the gardens at Dyrham and fourteen years old when Stephen Switzer described them in the *Ichnographia Rustica.* In Kip's print, on the left hand side of the mansion, is a 'wilderness' on the hillside. This is a garden maze of paths cut through high hedges. Switzer wrote essays for Jacobean and Stuart gardeners in which he sought to introduce 'irregularities' into landscape design. In spite of his predilection for a more natural landscape, his account suggests that he was impressed by the gardens at Dyrham. In 1718 he described walking through the wilderness thus:

(78

42

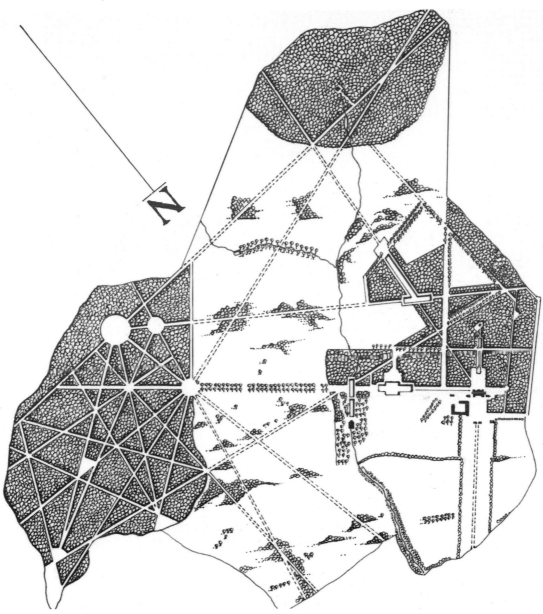

*you descend again to a flourishing Wilderness, on an easy Slope, cut out into the utmost Variety of Walkes, especially solitary Walks, and beautified with statues. In the middle there is a delightful square Garden, ... from whence your Prospect terminates in a large old Church at a very great Distance. I never in my whole Life did see so agreeable a Place...*

*The walks and rides in the woods in Bramham Park create glimpses beyond*

A similar 'wilderness' survived until recently at Bramham Park, near Leeds in Yorkshire. Here was the only large formal garden left in England until the wilderness of high beech hedges was destroyed in a storm in 1962. The first work credited to John Wood is in the gardens of Lord Bingley on the Bramham Park estate, where he prepared a survey of the great park and assisted in constructing buildings in the grounds.

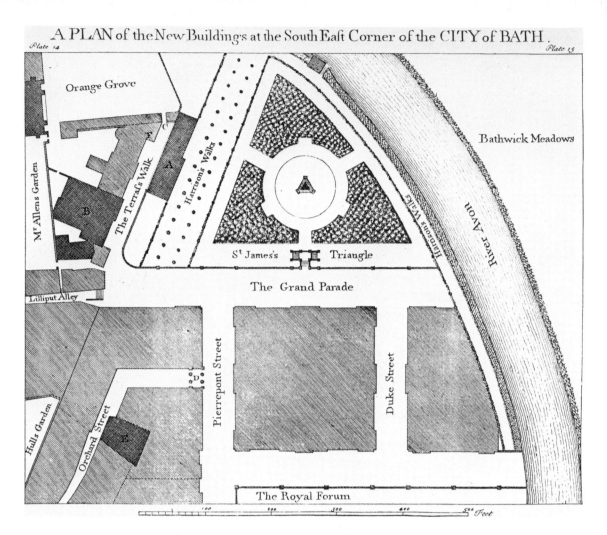

A PLAN of the New Buildings at the South East Corner of the CITY of BATH.

Plate 14
Plate 15

Orange Grove

Mr Allen's Garden

The Terra's Walk

Harrison's Walks

A

B

C

F

Lilliput Alley

Bathwick Meadows

River Avon

Harrison's Walks

St James's        Triangle

The Grand Parade

Pierrepont Street

Duke Street

Hull's Garden

Orchard Street

D

E

The Royal Forum

100    200    300    400    500 Feet

*A geometric design for hedges in Wood's proposals for St. James's Triangle*

How much was John Wood's architecture influenced by his early work at Bramham Park? As well as the formal garden in Queen Square, we find in his drawing of 1740, a pattern in St. James's Triangle, with three entrances to a circle within a triangle of hedges. Here is a solution to the geometric problem of designing with a triangle. It is an essay of three sides and three entrance points, but Wood must have been aware of what he was doing and the effect of passing through such a pattern of hedges. The high beech hedges really are a 'maze' only providing glimpses outwards from the centre when you turn, and this creates a particular architectural experience. These occasional glimpses, only visible when the observer moves around, are the basis of the outstanding|success of the enclosed space. A circle with four entrances would not have had the same effect. Here we see a garden design anticipating his scheme for the Circus, surely based on his experiences at Bramham Park.

Unlike at Queen Square, John Wood was able to level the ground of the Circus site and he lived long enough to set it out and see the foundation stone laid in 1754, but not to see his design completed. Building work began in 1755 and finished under the supervision of his son in 1766. The centre of

the Circus, however, never was laid out as a garden. The prints of Grimm in 1773 and Malton in 1780 show a paved space, with a reservoir in the centre and a lone watchman's box near to the Gay Street entrance. Cozens' print shows one of the glimpses down Gay Street to Beechen Cliff. The designs of the three curved terrace segments which make up the whole composition were probably also prepared by John Wood the younger. These depart from the austere Palladian discipline of his father and make no attempt at creating the symmetrical and formal palace but are exquisitely handled and detailed with the more theatrical style of a Roman amphitheatre.

*The Circus was originally paved (Cozens' print, 1773)*

However, the masterpiece of the younger John Wood must surely be the Royal Crescent. It has been suggested that the plan for the Crescent has classical precedents, being half of the Colosseum. Walter Ison suggests "there is a closer source to be found in Palladio's Teatro Olimpico, where the semi-elliptical auditorium is backed by an impressive colonnade of the same form". However, he also observes that the order that Wood employed for the Crescent's colonnade was the engaged Ionic order that his father had also used for the portico on the south front of Prior Park. Like his father's designs for the 'country mansion' at Prior Park, by mixing buildings and spaces, he created a palace in a rural rather than an urban setting. His father was influenced in his design for Queen Square by the classical geometrical design of earlier gardens and introduced a parterre into an urban setting. His son, however, was a contemporary of Capability Brown and, according to Dorothy Stroud, they worked together on the Kelston Estate at about the same time as the first foundation stone was laid in the Crescent.

45

*The Royal Crescent rising above an agricultural setting (Cozens' print, 1773)*

The Royal Crescent is, says Ison, "beyond question the summit of the Palladian achievement in Bath". It provides a magnificent climax to the sequence of designs which start from Queen Square. Its success is largely dependent on its setting. Here the scale of the sweep in the curve requires a substantial open space. This was available in the fields in which they were constructed and the pastures are shown in the print by Cozens and a 1793 watercolour by Grimm. When first constructed, its residents would have had a more or less uninterrupted view to the river and beyond to Beechen Cliff but according to William Watts in 1817 this view included buildings:

> *Immediately in front* [of the crescent] *lie what are Crescent Fields, gradually decking to a rich valley, through which the Avon flows towards the Severn, while the distance is closed by a variety of finely wooded and fertile hills, many of which are now covered with buildings.*

Although the Crescent is shorter than the span of the Prior Park mansion, it gives the appearance of a similar large country mansion in rural surroundings. The architects of the Palladian movement created country houses and even urban terraces which dominated their immediate landscape. Palladio's clients for villas were successful countrymen, farmers of the Veneto, who had tamed and cultivated the countryside. They were

proud of their success and, writes James Ackerman, "looked on nature with suspicion unless it had been tamed by man". Accordingly they asked for designs for villas which dominated the landscape. By the middle of the eighteenth century, the English country house was becoming part of the landscape instead of dominating it as at Prior Park.

Wood's Royal Crescent is carefully sited within the landscape and this is essential to the success of the building which rises from what is now a gently sloping lawn. This space was perhaps the only response that there could be to the scale and monumental style of the building. It was also in keeping with the, by then, fashionable landscapes of Capability Brown. By abandoning a formal garden in the front of a building, such as at Queen Square, Wood shows a very different approach from that of his father. Pevsner says of the Royal Crescent, "Nature is no longer the servant of architecture. The two are equals. The Romantic Movement is at hand".

*The Royal Crescent seen from the river (Watt's print, 1794)*

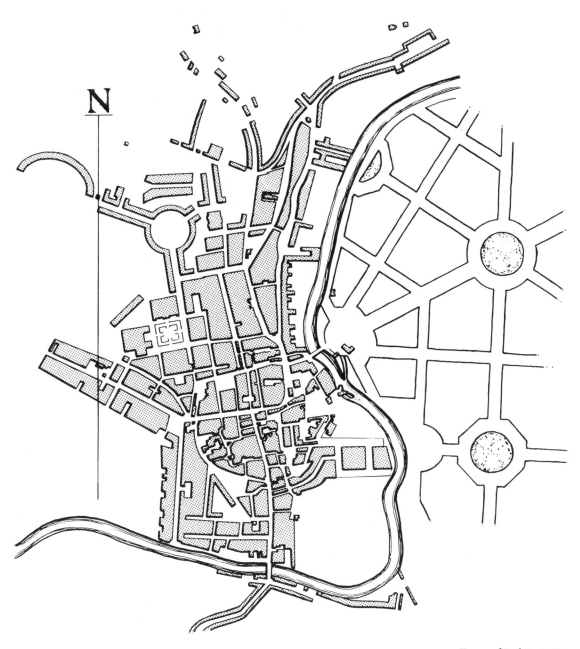

N

*Extent of Bath in 1772
with Adam's unrealised
proposals for Bathwick*

## 1

*Long suburbs extend now on every side of the city, and the meads on the opposite side of the river, which when the Parades were built, justified the motto upon one of the houses, 'Rus in Urbe', are now covered with another town.*

Robert Southey
*Letters from England*, 1807

# 5 Romantic Bathwick

Romanticism in literature, painting and other arts, emerges for the first time during the middle of the eighteenth century. In architecture it is expressed in the two styles; 'Classical Revival' and the 'Picturesque'. The first followed the work of the Adam brothers and William Chambers, and used results of more intensive studies of monuments of antiquity to produce buildings generally with a greater variety of classical motifs and more moulding of the facades. These buildings tended to be more massive than their predecessors and were in this way consistent with eighteenth century appreciation of the 'sublime' in matters of taste. The Picturesque Movement, however, was more closely related to debates on taste in landscape and it adopted a variety of architectural styles. Buildings were usually in an asymmetric form so that they could contribute more to a 'picturesque landscape'. Both of these architectural approaches contributed in different ways to the form of suburban Bath towards the end of the eighteenth century and thereby determined the character of its landscape.

By the time that the last of the Woods' developments in Bath had been completed, a period of frenetic building activity in the city had grown from a slow beginning and had died down. This activity extended the city to the north and west, where the land was not only steeper, but in a number of ownerships and thus prevented the completion of a comprehensive plan. The Woods had achieved some sort of unity by linking their developments, but elsewhere any unity of small developments could only be achieved with a common architectural style and materials. The largest estate in the city, however, lay on the eastern, Bathwick side of the river where flat land presented an opportunity for it to be developed easily to one overall design and layout. Robert Adam prepared proposals for what would have been the largest development in Bath, using neo-classical designs radiating across the meadows.

## 2

In 1769 William Johnstone Pulteney set about developing the Bathwick property he inherited from his wife's uncle, William Pulteney (Earl of Bath). In order to secure better rents on the estate when developed, Pulteney proposed to build a new bridge close to the city centre. This project required the co-operation of the city fathers, who were eventually persuaded to release land on their side of the river to secure the necessary bridgehead. After a protracted start with other architects, Pulteney

## 3

*Elizabeth Crossley's print shows Spring Gardens in the fields of Bathwick in 1760*

commissioned the Adam brothers to design and build the bridge. It was built by Robert Adam in early 1774, a year before the completion of the Royal Crescent, and coincided with the end of a brief boom in building.

One of the reasons for delay in the completion of the bridge and the proposed development of his estate was Pulteney's intention to provide a new turnpike road through his estate, out to a second bridge over the Avon and onto the London Road at Bathford. The new road would provide an opportunity to increase the rents on the estate and also provide an income from the tolls. The Trustees of the Turnpike Trust for the existing London Road objected to Pulteney's private Act of Parliament and the scheme was eventually lost. The delays, however, had a serious effect on the development of Bathwick. By the time the bridge was completed, the building boom was over and the American War of Independence had started. This colonial struggle lasted from 1775 to 1783 when investment and building materials, such as timber, were withdrawn from the building market throughout the country and redirected to the war effort.

If Pulteney was unlucky, he remained optimistic and commissioned Robert Adam to prepare designs for the new estate. His sketches were submitted in 1777, with more detailed drawings in 1782. Had the scheme been pursued, it would have created a development addressed to the river for the first time. The sketches show a very urban development and may (9 have borne in mind the similar water-front development of the Adelphi Terrace in London, which he and his brothers started in 1769. Both this and the suggested Bathwick development included residential buildings above basement wharfs along the riverside. Adam's scheme would have created a very grand neo-classical network of urban streets with terraces decorated with architectural motifs similar to the pilasters and domes on the bridge.

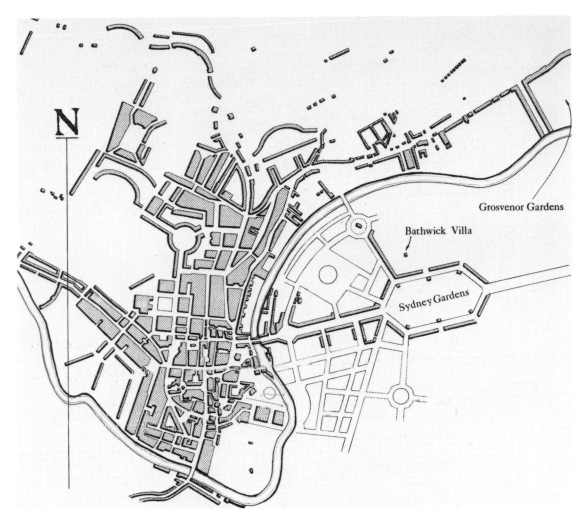

Grosvenor Gardens

Bathwick Villa

Sydney Gardens

The building market did not revive until 1788. Although Adam had submitted revised proposals earlier in 1782, these were not taken up by Pulteney's daughter, Henrietta Laura, to whom the estate had passed on Pulteney's death. Thomas Baldwin was now commissioned to design a layout for the estate and elevations of the buildings. He produced an impressive layout with a striking main street, Great Pulteney Street, reaching from the bridgehead at Argyle Street to the present Holburne of Menstrie Museum, but his elevations of the terraces are less impressive. Even Baldwin's contemporary, Thomas Telford, was critical:

*Baldwin's proposals for Bathwick shown on a map of Bath in 1793*

> *In Lady Bath's new town every circumstance was most fortunately combined... and yet I am sorry to say that I shall be able only to allow that there have been Streets and Squares and Crescents and Houses which a demand has forced, but alas - the Architect is not to be found.*

5)

Unlike earlier terraces by the Woods, Baldwin's designs did not relate to a landscaped area or feature with the possible exception of Barrow Hill above Twerton which aligns with Great Pulteney Street. At some stage

Great Pulteney Street was lined with trees but these have been removed and only a few remain in Laura Place. The open character of the area surrounding Great Pulteney Street is entirely fortuitous and not intended by Baldwin or Harcourt Masters, who proposed additional streets and squares for the estate. Bankruptcy overtook Baldwin, and many other architects, with the failure of the Bath Bank in 1793, and work on this estate and elsewhere was halted and further delayed by the depression of the building market caused by the first of the Napoleonic Wars.

The *Historical and Local New Bath Guide* of 1802 noted the depressed state of the market due to the 'desolating hand of war' and hoped

> *the auspicious return of Peace to this country, which has deeply mourned her long absence, and the loss of her benign influence, will arouse in the breasts of some worthy persons, the spirit of enterprise and induce them to execute the design formed, and commenced about ten years ago, the building of a square, two new crescents, and street contiguous to London Road...* (96)

Contemporary maps indicate the location of the proposed streets and squares but when peace did eventually return, and some new building took place with terraces by John Pinch in the Sydney Gardens area, much of the proposed Bathwick Estate remained unbuilt. The open spaces of Henrietta Park and the Recreation Ground have survived but remained meadow land until the nineteenth century. Baldwin's proposals for the Bathwick Estate included the construction of new pleasure gardens in a large hexagon around which terraced houses would be built. The gardens would offer a place of entertainment and refreshment similar to those offered in Ranelagh and Vauxhall in London. The development of Sydney Gardens was one of the largest and most successful of such schemes, but it was by no means the first.

Bath had become a fashionable resort from the beginning of the eighteenth century but never offered more than a limited amount of attractions out of doors. The earliest pleasure gardens were formed by Thomas Harrison who in 1708 provided private walks and "Gardens for People of Rank and Fortune to walk in" alongside his Assembly Rooms. (97) Here formal gardens extended to the river and can be seen on the early prints and maps by the Buck brothers and Wood. Later a bowling green was laid out on the site of Wood's proposed Circus. As the city developed, alternative attractions were sought so that by the time Thorpe prepared his plan in 1742, as well as the gardens in Lyncombe, a rival establishment of Spring Gardens appears to have been set up on the site of an earlier house. Sydenham records a letter writer in 1753 who described this garden as "the fair Elysium of this place where sweet variety tempts every sense to rapture". By 1769 these Gardens were advertised as a 'Vauxhall'. Here at (98) first patrons could only be tempted to the refreshments and other events such as balls and concerts after walking round past Widcombe or after using a river ferry boat from Slippery Lane.

For a while, one of the few reasons for using the completed Pulteney Bridge was to go to either Spring Gardens or the prison. Sydenham also notes that pedestrians were permitted across whilst the bridge was being built for according to a notice in 1772 "chairs and foot passengers may pass over the New Bridge during the Races [on Claverton Down] but no horses

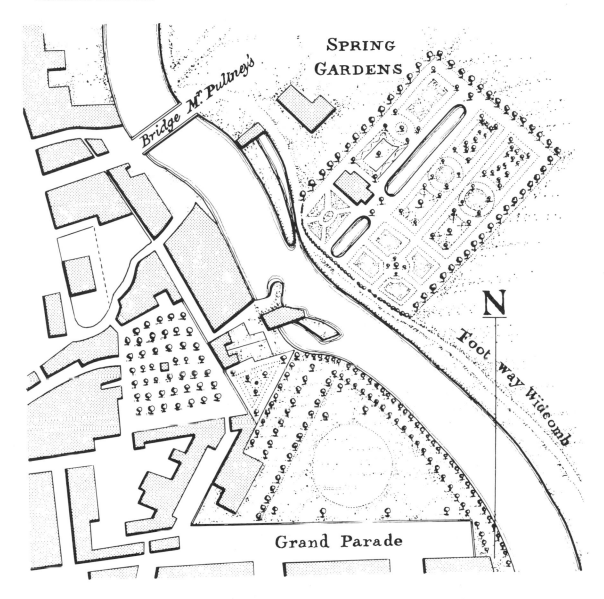

SPRING
GARDENS

Bridge Mr Pulteney's

N

Foot way Widcomb

Grand Parade

99) or carriages as the Way is not Pitched". The development of the Bathwick
Estate ruined the setting and privacy of these gardens and in 1795 they
closed to become a builder's yard for John Eveleigh, after the more
formidable rival in Sydney Gardens had opened.

*Spring Gardens in 1772
laid out with a 'canal'
and formal gardens*

    Another pleasure garden that has now gone, was on fields north of
Sydney Gardens. The land was bought in 1777 by a Mr. James Ferry who
built a gothic style 'Bathwick Villa', very similar in style to the Countess of
Huntingdon's Chapel in the Vineyards. The Villa and garden were opened
to the public and described by Fanny Burney in June 1780 as a "very curious
house and garden". It appears that the gothic style was not to Miss Burney's
taste for she thought Mr. Ferry had made "unsuccessful attempts at making
00) something of nothing". However, the gardens were to survive her visit by
another ten years. When they were auctioned in April 1782, they were

53

*The Hotel, now Grosvenor House, is all that remains of the Grosvenor Gardens Vauxhall*

described as:

> *...commanding many beautiful views of Bath and the country circumjacent. The Gardens consist of about an acre and a quarter, laid out in modern taste with serpentine gravel walks, valuable shrubbery, evergreens, fishponds, bridges, fruit trees in the highest perfection.* (10

After the auction, a subscription garden was opened in July 1783 and advertised in the 1786 *Bath Guide Book* as a public tea garden. The new proprietor, Mr. Marrett, a merchant offering more than tea, "...begs leave to inform the Nobility and Gentry and the public in general, that he has imported a stock of choice French wines..." The admission ticket refers to (10 the availability of neat wines, but Marrett also provided concerts, fireworks and other illuminations. Unfortunately, these attractions were far from the centre of the city and, like the Spring Gardens, affected by the Bathwick building operations, they closed in 1790. The name for the area remained on various maps as Villa Fields until the villa was demolished in 1897 and the area built over.

A more ambitious project was built outside Bathwick on the other side of the river bank from Villa Fields. Here Eveleigh planned and started constructing the Grosvenor Gardens Vauxhall. This project started a year after the demise of Bathwick Villa in 1791, when building leases were let and "the centre of the Meadows to be laid out as Pleasure Gardens". In (10 June 1791 the foundation stone of an hotel was laid for the building which has subsequently become Grosvenor House. With the exception of Adam's

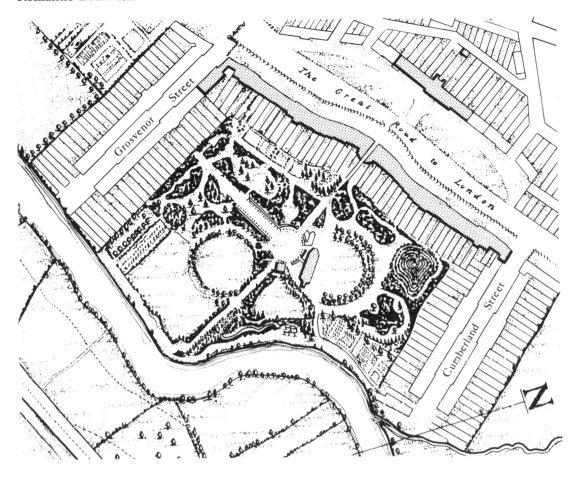

frustrated scheme for Bathwick, Eveleigh's development is the first to be built, or at least started, where the design addresses the river and it is, so far, the only major development to have done so. Here Eveleigh proposed a Vauxhall Garden which took advantage of the river, not just as part of the design but as a means of getting to the Gardens by boat from the city centre. Unlike Bathwick Villa, Eveleigh's designs for the riverside gardens have been recorded on contemporary maps and show a variety of entertainments in a landscaped setting, with bowling greens, labyrinths and firework displays all linked with gravel walks. The map makers also showed the proposed surrounding terraces in Grosvenor Street and Cumberland Street. But their confidence was, in the event, misplaced, because in 1793, with the crash of the Bath Bank, Eveleigh too was declared bankrupt and his planned development abandoned. Later the Gardens were revived for a brief period but they and the remaining development were eventually abandoned for good. After remaining in horticultural use the site was eventually built on for very modest suburban housing in the 1960s.

*Grosvenor Gardens from a map of 1808 shown with adjacent but never completed terraces*

The failure of the Bath Bank affected a number of building projects throughout the city. As I have mentioned, Baldwin was also a victim, but not before he promoted the more successful pleasure garden at Sydney Gardens. In spite of the considerable difficulties caused by the failure of

*A Victorian view of some of the delights of Sydney Gardens*

the bank, he was even advertising with designs for an hotel for tenders from builders a year later. The hotel was eventually completed, after the gardens opened, by Charles Harcourt Masters with a similar design.

Sydney Gardens with sixteen acres was larger and more ambitious than any of the other attempts at creating a Vauxhall and has survived more or less to this day even after some changes and encroachments by the Kennet and Avon Canal Company and the Great Western Railway. Both of these operators were required to provide with their undertaking some picturesque accommodation works such as walls or bridges. The gardens were originally privately owned and offered a number of entertainments to subscribers. By 1801 the *New Bath Guide* described them as containing

> *a great number of small delightful groves, pleasant vistas, and charming lawns intersected by serpentine walks, which at every turn meet with sweet, shady bowers, furnished with handsome seats, some composed by nature, others by art. It is decorated by waterfalls, stone and thatched pavilions, alcoves; the Kennet and Avon Canal running through with two elegant cast-iron bridges thrown over it, after the manner of the Chinese, a sham castle planted with several pieces of cannon, bowling greens, swings, a labyrinth formed by enclosed pathways, the principal one of which, after many intricate windings, leads to fine Merlin Swing, and a grotto of antique appearance. . .*

(10

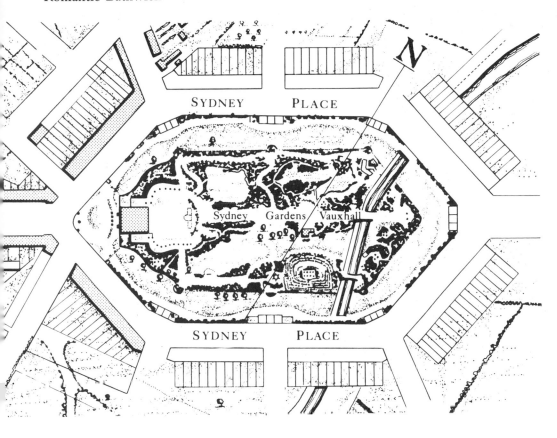

SYDNEY PLACE

Sydney Gardens Vauxhall

N

SYDNEY PLACE

The neo-classical architecture of Bathwick Estate created an urban landscape of terraces and streets laid out in formal arrangements. Although not all of the planned circuses and squares were built, the success of the estate lay in the formalizing of the concept of the earlier pleasure garden in Sydney Gardens. Here terraces were proposed, arranged around a large garden or park. These terraces influenced contemporary schemes elsewhere; perhaps the most significant contained John Nash's proposals for Regent's Park in London. Not only were Bath's crescents and circuses reflected in his designs but also the Sydney Gardens concept of terraces laid out around a park. Both of these parks have a canal crossing the park. Nash wrote of Regents Park "many persons would consider the circumstance of 5) Boats and Barges passing along the canal as enlivening the scenery". Canals were in accord with the spirit of the 'picturesque'. The *Bath Chronicle* in 1801 agreed:

*Sydney Gardens Vauxhall from a map of 1808 shown with proposed terraces*

> *The novelty of the Kennet and Avon Canal, which is carried through the Garden and Ride, and compleated in the most handsome manner, with Ornamental Iron Bridges etc. with various Improvements in the Plantations, add considerably to the Picturesque Beauties for which the* 6) *Spot has been so universally admired.*

57

*The picturesque setting of Camden Place (print of 1794)*

*...as such buildings depart from regularity, they now and then acquire something of scenery, which I should think might not unsuccessfully be adapted by an architect...*

Joshua Reynolds
*Thirteenth Discourse*, 1786

# 6   Picturesque Lansdown

The "Picturesque Beauties" of Sydney Gardens were created, in part, by a variety of eclectic but fashionable and romantic additions to the gardens. The odd collection of thatched cottages, Chinese inspired bridges and a sham castle are entirely different from the classical discipline of Adam's and Baldwin's architecture, but both are products of the Romantic Movement. The Classical Revival style of Adam and his successors broke free from the more severe and rigid discipline of Palladian Architecture, although as Pevsner points out, Adam did not often depart from Palladian standards on the exteriors of his country houses. Practitioners of the Revival used a more delicate and decorated architecture with details and decorative motifs gleaned from classical antiquity. The other popular expression of the Romantic Movement is the Picturesque with the revival of medieval forms in the development of 'Gothic' architecture. Kenneth Clark has argued that English Gothic never died in the English Renaissance because medieval styles constantly reappear in buildings during the seventeenth and eighteenth centuries. The eighteenth century Romanticism combined a renewed interest in the medieval and gothic antiquity with the fashionable conception of the landscape garden, to create the 'Picturesque' style.

The first published use of the term 'picturesque' occurs in 1768 in an *Essay on Prints* written by Rev. William Gilpin. Here he defined the idea as "that kind of beauty which would look well in a picture". Gilpin was encouraged by the poet, Thomas Gray, who had started out in 1739 on a European Grand Tour with Horace Walpole and had published an account of the English Lakes in 1775. Gilpin followed this with descriptions of his own tours in the country including an account of the River Wye in 1782, the Lake District in 1786 and the Highlands in 1789. In the same way that the Adam brothers and other architects completed a Grand Tour of Europe and returned excited by the classical architecture and ruins they had seen and sketched, other young men had returned excited by the drama of the landscape through which they had passed, particularly that of the wild Alps and northern Italy.

The paintings that they brought back showed temples, grottoes and ruins in a 'dramatic landscape'. Whilst the neo-classical architects returned to recreate the classical buildings they had seen, others were content to return and recreate the classical ruins, and classical landscape.

From the middle of the eighteenth century, Capability Brown was producing a more placid and somnolent landscape which proved to be too subtle for many who were moved by the more savage scenery they had seen on the Grand Tour. Kenneth Clark notes:

> ...the fact remains that when an ordinary traveller of the sixteenth and seventeenth centuries crossed the Alps it never occurred to him to admire the scenery - until the year 1739, when the poet Thomas Gray, visiting the Grande Chartreuse, wrote in a letter: 'Not a precipice, not a torrent, not a cliff, but is pregnant with religion and poetry'. Amazing! Might have been Ruskin. (1

As travel became easier, travel books such as those by Gilpin and Gray popularised the wilder natural beauty of nearer home and in particular the Lake District, Wales and Scotland. Some of this popularity will have been due to the effective closure of large parts of Europe to English travellers during the Napoleonic Wars. The vogue for the picturesque enthusiast like William Gilpin, whose numerous books on the subject are important documents in taste, affected the landscape at large rather than in the garden. (11

Whilst the term picturesque was applied initially to landscape it also gradually came to be applied to architectural style. Considerable effort had been spent in adapting or levelling a site and surrounding landscape to accommodate the rigid discipline of a Palladian building. The Picturesque approach was to encourage a building to sit in its surroundings, providing not only a different landscape setting but breaking away from the rigid discipline of the Palladian style. Richard Payne Knight had sought to define picturesque, explaining that it meant the

> blending and melting of objects together with a playful and airy lightness and a sort of loose sketchy indistinctness. (1

In the same way that post-Adam architects provided a more liberated classical architecture by drawing from a wider range of classical sources, so did the architects of the picturesque draw not only from antiquity, but also from a wider range of styles. William Kent had been pursuing earlier gothic architecture at the beginning of the century but Sanderson Miller and Horace Walpole developed and popularised the Chinese buildings and gardens and, later, Indian styles were explored with buildings at Sezincote by S.P. Cockerell and the Brighton Pavilion by John Nash.

The Picturesque Movement, however, can conveniently be said to start at the same time as the first Napoleonic War in 1794 with the publication of three books. Payne Knight published *The Landscape, a Didactic Poem* and Uvedale Price provided an *Essay on the Picturesque*. The following year Humphrey Repton published *Sketches and Hints on the Landscape Garden*. These books put forward the thesis that 'quality' should be studied with constant reference to the landscape and that the landscape of every site had character and features which should be highlighted and reinforced. In Bath, however, it is not so easy to define the emergence of the Romantic or

*The picturesque folly of Sham Castle built in 1755*

Picturesque Movements. Ralph Allen had been building grottoes, temples and other features and furniture in his garden at Prior Park from 1741. Ten years later a more substantial gothic building was built at Lacock Abbey by Sanderson Miller.

This Warwickshire architect had built a castellated gothic ruin near his own house at Edgehill in 1745 and a sham ruin at Hagley in 1747. Either John Wood or Ralph Allen had decided that a gothic ruin was needed in Bath. William Pitt, who was a capable gardener as well as a politician, assisted by inviting Sanderson Miller to design a ruin for Allen. The result, Sham Castle, was eventually built by Allen's Clerk of Works in 1762. Although the design is now attributed to Sanderson Miller, Richard Jones claims it to be his own:

> *Built the Castle on the warren to my design, but I would have built it larger, for an object to be seen further off but was hindered by my master and other gentlemen.*

The gothic castle is only a folly, an 'eye-catcher' on the edge of Bathampton Down, and was designed with the intention of being seen at its best effect from the windows of Allen's town house in Lilliput Alley near Abbey Green. This building marks the beginning of the 'Romantic Movement' in Bath for both architectural styles and landscape 'improvement'.

61

The steep hills around Bath offered excellent opportunities to site romantic ruins according to the rules of taste and principles of the Picturesque Movement. These qualities were not lost on the author of the *Bath Guide* of 1802 who noted that:

> *Lansdown is one of the most conspicuous and happily situated hills in the West of England, it commands the most enchanting and interesting views; from hence can be seen the bosoms of Somersetshire, Gloucestershire, Worcestershire and Wiltshire, elegantly diversified with hills swelling over hills, vales and intersecting vales, rivers meeting rivers, towns and villages with their towering spires, villas, groves etc; far distant appears the sea rolling her waves, by the lofty mountains of Wales. All these unite to fill the soul with indescribable transports of delight.* (11

The steepness of the upper slopes also created problems in maintaining the Palladian discpline and designing classical and symmetrical buildings similar to those that had been built lower down on the more gentle slopes. A new generation of crescents and terraces emerged above the city taking advantage of their sites after abandoning any attempt at symmetry or a formal layout as at St. James's Square. John Summerson considers such well-sited crescents irresistable:

> *On steep sites they sink comfortably into the hillsides; by the sea they give a happy suggestion of panoramic vision; and where there is neither hill nor sea they still possess an elegance and humanity denied to the straight terrace or the awesome and too embracing curves.* (11

As if to demonstrate the difficulty of allocating convenient periods to styles of architecture and landscape gardening, the subsequent developments closest to the Royal Crescent consisted of straight forward terraces and two squares. St. James's Square is similar in size to Queen Square but far less impressive. It was built on the site of gardens used by tenants of the Royal Crescent, one of which was Christopher Anstey, who had to transplant his beech trees to Shockerwick and objected to being evicted from his much loved garden with the following epigram:

> *Ye men of Bath, who stately mansions rear*
> *To wait for tenants from Lord knows where,*
> *Would you pursue a plan that cannot fail,*
> *Erect a mad house and enlarge your gaol.* (1

The Square remains, with the nearby Catherine Place, a charming but suburban square. Pevsner notes that the picturesque "entered the town not in urban terms. About 1800 the first squares of London were landscaped exclaves of country in the town". (1

The nearby Portland Place of 1786 is a well mannered symmetrical terrace sitting rather uncomfortably above Burlington Street. This and the adjacent terraces are well designed and for the most part cope well with the difficulty of taking terraces along and up the hills, but make no concession to the contour and are not the execution of an overall plan. These were built by local architects and business men who were meeting the demand of a

*Camden Place presented for a while an unintentional but picturesque ruin (Nattes' print, 1806)*

0)

1)

shortlived boom for housing during the brief interlude between the American War and the Napoleonic Wars. As R.S. Neale and C.W. Chalkin have shown, many of the men who invested in property and such speculative ventures at this time were craftsmen or tradesmen associated with the building industry. They could use their experience and, in the case of St. James's Square, their skills.

Not all of the ventures were well advised and some rash decisions ended in disaster. One of the first terraces to be built higher up the hills, taking advantage of the contours to make the best of a 'picturesque' site, is Camden Place. This was designed by the ill-fated Eveleigh, who proposed a magnificent curved terrace which would have matched the scale of the Royal Crescent, albeit curving more gently along the slopes of Lansdown. The rather quirky classical design was, however, based on poor foundations and alas, before the construction work was finished, the eastern end of the terrace slipped away in a landslide and was never completed. Although poor Eveleigh never intended this particular picturesque effect the remaining ruins provided a subject for dramatic and surreal prints of a classical and apparently partly ruined building rising high above the river. This image captured the essential drama of the picturesque.

More successful in many ways than Camden Place is its near neighbour Lansdown Crescent. This was designed and built by John Palmer in 1789-93. The intriguing serpentine form of the crescent clings to the contour of the hills with the terrace rising above a very steeply sloping open

63

space. This field is too steep to be treated like the lawn in front of the Royal Crescent and to this day is pastoral, being grazed as always by sheep. Comparison with the Royal Crescent which rises from a gentle 'Brownian' landscape is interesting for if that Crescent is beautiful, then Lansdown Crescent is sublime.

The middle of the eighteenth century was the age of the 'Enlightenment' when intellectual enquiry extended from scientific and philosophical reason into the arts and matters of taste. What was considered to be sublime or beautiful was investigated by Edmund Burke in 1759. He argued that

> *sublime objects are vast in their dimensions, beautiful ones comparatively small; beauty should be smooth, and polished; the great rugged, and negligent; beauty should shun the right line, yet deviate from it insensibly; the great in many cases loves the right line, and when it deviates, it often makes a strong deviation.*

(1

A better idea of the right line was set out in an essay by William Hogarth in 1753, *The Analysis of Beauty* written with a view of fixing the fluctuating Ideas of Taste. It was much criticised by those of his contemporaries who considered themselves sole arbiters of taste. Hogarth repudiated these connoisseurs of art and their styles which

dominated the art and literature of the period. He was not wed to "the rules and perpetuation of order in art but to the naturalness and the limited variety to be found in life itself". In the *The Analysis of Beauty*, Hogarth identified the 'line of Beauty':

*Hogarth's print from the 'Analysis of Beauty'*

> *...though all sorts of waving lines are ornamental, when properly applied; yet strictly speaking, there is one precise line properly called the line of beauty.*

Hogarth drew a series of sinuous lines on a plate for the essay and defined one of these lines, which was neither too slight nor too curved, as a 'line of beauty'. Pevsner suggests that this gentle double curve dominates English art from the ogee of the Decorated style of medieval architecture to William Blake and beyond. Hogarth would have been familiar with the significance of such a serpentine line to English Architecture and English Gardening because he had worked for a period under Kent. However, in his essay, Hogarth compared the various lines with legs of chairs, curves on animals' horns and ladies' corsets. He may have been more impressed if he had been able to compare the lines with John Palmer's plan for Lansdown Place and Crescent. Here the sinuous curves of the crescent are remarkably close to Hogarth's 'line of beauty'.

Part of the effect of the Crescent stems from the long gentle, double curve which has clearly been 'properly applied' and in Hogarth's words, which come from garden design, "lead the eye in a wanton kind of chase" and thereby introduces those elements of surprise sought by Pope in the composition of an English Garden:

65

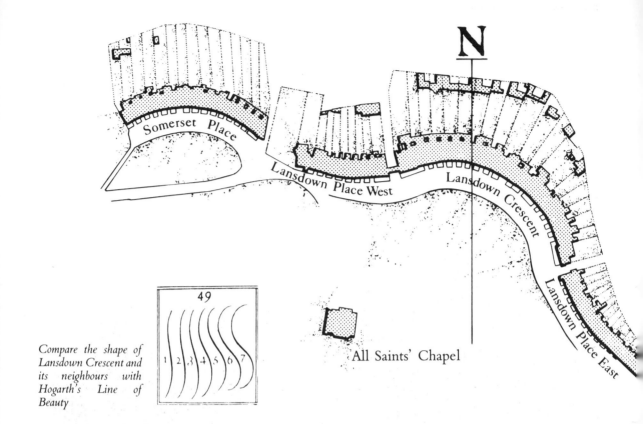

*Compare the shape of Lansdown Crescent and its neighbours with Hogarth's Line of Beauty*

*Let not each beauty everywhere be spied*
*When half the skill is decently to hide.*
*He gains all points who pleasingly confounds,*
*Surprises, varies, and conceals the bounds.*

Palmer must gain some of these points with the Crescent which hides and surprises us by curving round the hill and dropping down to a further building at its western end. It used to enclose a 'Gothic' church, All Saints' Chapel, in the bosky open space below. The additional terrace at its western end, Somerset Place, however, was designed by different architects. This curious terrace was originally designed and built as a semi-detached building which survives in the centre of the crescent. Its architectural style differs from that of Lansdown Crescent but it does provide a complementary and logical extension. The broken pediment above the central pair of houses may serve as an epitaph to Eveleigh's broken heart, because this development, along with Grosvenor Place, was not completed following the failure of the Bath Bank in 1793 and it remained unfinished until the 1820s.

The Napoleonic Wars can be regarded as a convenient start to the Picturesque Movement but they also marked the decline of Bath's fortunes as a fashionable spa and resort. The failure of the Bath Bank was more than a local crisis affecting the city's builders and thereby delaying the completion of some building schemes; it marked the beginning of a more profound

change in the role and character of the city. The French Revolutionary and *The still incomplete* Napoleonic Wars lasted from February 1793 to November 1815, with a *Lansdown Place above* brief respite in the period of truce offered by the Treaty of Amiens in 1802. *All Saint's Church in* After a peak in 1792, the numbers of visitors fell off and only regained their *1792* former levels in the boom years of the 1820s. Not only was this change a result of rising costs and changes in fashion, but by then Bath was beginning to suffer from the competition offered by other resorts such as Cheltenham and Brighton.

The crescents of Lansdown are a high point in the development of terraces in Bath. Here their architects moved away from the earlier formal layouts to more informal terraces snaking along the contours of the hillsides. These buildings use those characteristics of their sites which integrate them with their immediate landscapes. Not only have the architects created dramatic and picturesque designs but their buildings to this day contribute to the character of the present city and its landscape by retaining large areas of trees around the terraces. The decline of the city as a resort reduced the demand for terraces of large houses in the beginning of the nineteenth century. Because of this, from now on, the picturesque approach to buildings and landscape took on a new form in that of the Regency villa.

7)

*Detached villas below*
*the slopes of Lansdown*
*(from a print of 1844)*

## 28

*The City of Bath has so considerably increased in size and the number of inhabitants within the last thirty years, that it is now become one of the most agreeable, as well as the most polite places in the Kingdom; owing chiefly to the elegance of its buildings and the accommodations of strangers, which are superior to any other city in England.*

*Historical and Local New Bath Guide, 1802*

# 7      Suburban Villas

The decline of the city as a place of resort meant that it became instead a place of permanent residence. Consequently, the demand for lodging houses close to the centre declined and there was a greater demand for comfortable homes at the more salubrious edges of the city. Bath became for the first time a place attractive for retirement for an affluent middle class. The census figures for 1811 and 1821 show a significant increase in the proportion of elderly and female resident population. At the same time the censuses show that in spite of the decline of the city as a resort, its population continued to rise from some 33,000 recorded in 1801, by some 16% in 1811 and by a further 21% in 1821, to a total of 46,700.

Some of the increased population recorded in these censuses lived in increasingly squalid housing in the centre of the city, in the Dolemeads, in Holloway, and in Lyncombe. Alongside these crowded slums grew the new emerging industries and all were susceptible to the dangers of disasters from fire, flood and disease. This was not for the middle classes, however, who continued to build for themselves comfortable houses on the upper slopes at the outskirts of the city. A few of the pre-war projected developments were able to continue but there were not many new projects. The irony of the situation was pointed out by Bryan Little, for during the first quarter of the nineteenth century there was an improvement in those schemes that were completed, with the

*abandonment and frustration of over ambitious schemes which the Napoleonic Wars may have helped to kill... the work done is the logical fulfilment of lines already laid down. Strangely enough, there is at times a rallying in quality compared to much put up in the preceding quarter century.*

Although Southey declared in 1807 that "it is plain that Bath has outgrown its Beauty", there are examples of good and beautiful buildings in the villas in Lyncombe and Bathwick. Pinch and others were able to continue also with the construction of some terraces in Sydney Place and Cavendish and Widcombe Crescents. They are relatively few in number. The post-war developments brought a significant change in housing development with the growing popularity of the suburban villa. This form of housing was not a sudden new breakthrough in design but a logical fulfilment of one of the lines already laid down by the picturesque Movement. Summerson has described the intimate connection between the villa type of house and the informal landscape. The more formal Palladian design for a country house such as Prior Park was "conceived as a ruling element in a ruled environment. The villa on the contrary, was an object to be placed pictorially within a landscape". The development of dramatic terraces in Lansdown may have created an overall 'picturesque' landscape but whilst it was possible to curve these crescents around the hillside contours, it was very much easier, and cheaper, to site a smaller villa in its own landscape, and the semi-detached villa was a compromise between the terrace and the detached house. The substitution of semi-detached villas for the terrace, conceived as a single classical composition, is considered by Olive Cook to have completed the conquest of the Palladian order by the 'picturesque' style.

The development of the smaller 'picturesque' villa was not a sudden change, for it had its beginnings in the early years of the eighteenth century and its roots in antiquity. Many of the ancient Romans experienced the sentimental desire to enjoy or live in the countryside around their towns and cities. Letters of Pliny the Younger describe the accommodation offered by a 'villa suburbana' which was more of a country retreat for pleasure than a home. Later the Italian Renaissance produced similar buildings with the Palazzo del Te, and Palladio even attempted to reconstruct a building as described by Pliny with the Villa Madama. However, many of Palladio's villas built for his clients of the Veneto, were estate houses for country gentlemen who were reclaiming agricultural land for sixteenth century Venice. Here, as Summerson points out, Palladio does not call these houses villas, "he calls them 'casa di villa' which allows to villa the meaning of a country estate".

Pope and his friends had taken to the concept of the villa and were one of the earliest groups to do so. They were enthusiastic gardeners and the garden or grounds of the suburban villa was an essential part of the formula for its success. It enabled the middle classes or bourgeoisie, who had no pretentions to being landlords, nor even enough money, to buy a dignified property. The building might be of a variety of styles, classical or gothic or even cottage orné but in all cases there was enough ground to provide a garden and a proper setting. Capability Brown showed no great interest in the villa but his successor, Humphrey Repton, lived at Hare Street in a small villa with a garden "which he landscaped with all the care that he might have lavished on his most grandiose stately house commission". Repton had turned to landscape work from when he was thirty-six years old to become the natural successor to Capability Brown. The 'Brownian' landscape had destroyed the distinction between the park and garden and had become too subtle for many tastes. Some of Brown's critics said that "he turned good agricultural land into half-hearted grazing", and he certainly did destroy many old gardens when he set the great houses floating in a sea of grass. Repton slowly reintroduced the idea of a garden with plants and flowers around the house. For country houses, such as Bowood, these gardens were sited immediately adjacent to the house with a 'Brownian' park behind.

Suburban Villas

Repton is not known to have worked in Bath but his influence on gardening of the day was considerable and this would have set a style for the landscape of the new suburban villas. He published books and articles on suburban villas and considered that there was a close link between the style of building and its garden even to the choice of trees. Disgusted by the choice of wrong trees such as the Lombardy Poplar, he wrote in 1816 of "spruce villas, surrounded by spruce firs, attended by Lombardy Poplars, profusely scattered over the face of the country". He was disgusted, too, when houses in the gothic style were surrounded by firs or Lombardy Poplars instead of by trees with a rounded outline.

Repton collaborated with the architect, John Nash, who is regarded by Summerson as the greatest figure in the whole Picturesque Movement.

> *His work embraces every aspect of it* [the Picturesque] *while there is nothing in his enormous oeuvre which does not illustrate it. It was he who popularised the irregular castellated house and the picturesque thatched cottage.*

Their partnership pioneered the development of housing estates with villas in a landscaped setting as at Park Village in Regent's Park. Repton had always liked

> *the cheerful village, the high road and that constant moving scene which I would not exchange for any of the lovely parks that I have improved for others.*

One of the most celebrated villages that Repton and Nash created was part of their improvement of the Harford family estate at Henbury, then just outside Bristol. Blaise Hamlet was to influence other contemporary improvements and in due course a whole tradition of urban planning. Here in 1811 they brought together what at first appears to be an almost casual and random collection of buildings but in fact is a very carefully considered and placed variety of designs of rustic cottages, similar to those being published in contemporary books and pamphlets. Blaise Hamlet was the prime example of the 'picturesque' village and 'romanticism' in a highly appropriate form.

The romantic simplicity and rustic character of the cottage orné became an acceptable style for suburban villas or structures within gardens and for lodges such as at the Paragon School in Lyncombe. Edward Davis in 1830 created the Farmhouse in Royal Victoria Park, emulating 'improved' farm estates built by landowners elsewhere. The suburban development of Regency Bath was speculative and not part of any improved estates nor the creation of new villages, although Pierce Egan noted in 1819 that at Lambridge is to be seen

> *a neat row of houses... with long gardens tastefully laid out in front of them. A few trees and hedges also intersect at various places the different houses, giving this part of it the air of an elegant village.*

As at Lambridge, most of the new villas spread out alongside the existing roads or on such hillsides as offered a 'picturesque' or 'romantic' setting. John

71

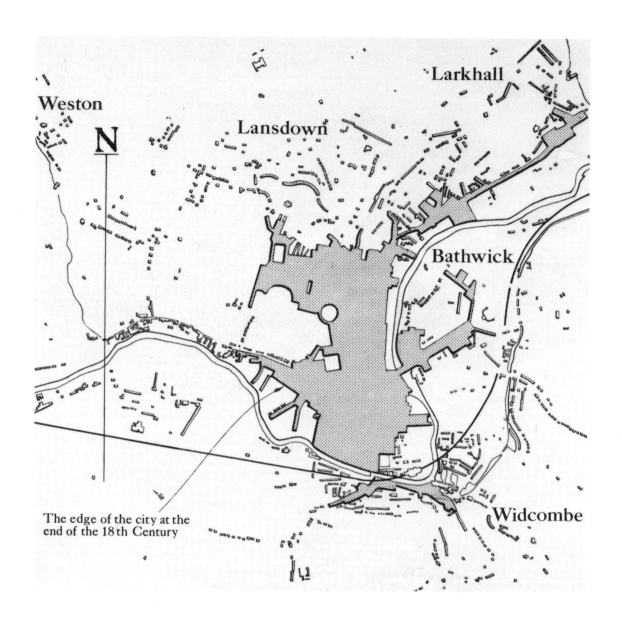

The edge of the city at the
end of the 18th Century

*Extent of the city in the middle of the 19th century (based on plans of 1851 and 1808)*

Britton noted in his 1830 edition of Anstey's *New Bath Guide* a description of Lyncombe which was a

> *romantic, narrow valley... which, in Anstey's time, was a rural, shady retreat. Now it has changed its features, and if not vilified, is villa-fied, by a profusion of cottage-ornees, mansions, gardens, etc. Although many of the valleys in the vicinity of this city abound with secluded and romantic beauties, that of Lincomb is pre-eminent. Hence it is not surprising that many of the citizens should resort to it as a place of domestic quiet, and suburban residence.*

(14

The term villa had, according to Summerson, taken on this suburban connotation by 1815. In Bath, however, it occurs earlier but less frequently, (14

Wood referring to villas in his *Description of Bath* in 1765 and Mary *Detached villas extend-* Chandler describing the views around the city in 1735 in which "Towns, *ing up Bathwick Hill* Rivers, Villas, Flocks and Herds appear". These villas may be truly rural rather than suburban. However, according to the papers of the Pulteney Estate, building the Pulteney Bridge in 1774 was partly justified by offering advantages to the future development of the Bathwick Area. "It is supposed too, that many of the inhabitants will choose to build villas along the face of the Hill as the situation and prospect are remarkably fine". Later in 1788, Baldwin advertised an unrealised project in a published set of his drawings, which included designs for houses some of which are referred to as villas.

In due course a line of villas was built between 1810 and 1825 along Bathwick Hill as Bryan Little writes:

> *...marking a frontier between the rugged ground above those breathlessly lovely, cow studded sheets of pastoral greenery below. Here the villas... are beautifully executed works, and of a great variety in detail, built no doubt to meet many individual tastes.*

The Bathwick villas have a garden around each house reaching to the adjacent fields, and all are rising above the city. They repeat, but on a smaller scale, the work that Repton was accomplishing in country houses elsewhere, until his death in 1818. They are large detached houses of a classical style and although John Claudius Loudon pointed out that "such

73

quasi rural living was unknown to the citizen of the Greek polis" many villas use Grecian motifs which had become increasingly fashionable in the Regency period. Cruikshank notes:

> Though dominant, the Greek revival did not hold absolute sway in the early nineteenth century house design. Other styles did emerge from the melting pot of the beginning of the century, and some flourished. Disparate as they were, they had in common the fact that more than most products of the Greek revival, they reflected the themes of the picturesque - asymmetry, romantic antiquity and rusticity...

In these small houses then, the classical tradition of Bath remains dominant. Consequently there are only few early Gothic Revival buildings in the city. The gothic style was one of several adopted by the architects of the Romantic Movement. Although, as Kenneth Clark has pointed out, as a style it had never really died out, the Revival made it fashionable again, particularly in the 1820s. The medieval european architecture was only referred to as gothic in the seventeenth century, probably at the time John Evelyn used the term 'Gottic'. The medieval gothic style is not only expressed in church architecture but in secular buildings. It was maintained in a tradition of building construction by provincial builders throughout the country. In the middle of the eighteenth century one or two notable buildings used the gothic style in a picturesque manner. As well as building sham castles, Sanderson Miller built a new hall at Lacock Abbey in 1753. About the same time Horace Walpole was building himself a large rambling house, Strawberry Hill at Twickenham.

Walpole became more confident of the merits of an irregularly designed building and was fond of the "want of symmetry in buildings as in the grounds or gardens". The gothic style offered the Romantic architect a rich source from 'medieval antiquity' but it provided the right sort of irregular architecture for a picturesque development. Kenneth Clark has observed that an essential characteristic of gothic buildings is that it is usually possible to walk round a medieval church, cathedral or castle. Richard Warner commented in 1800 that the Chapel in Holloway "...a neat gothic building and elegantly hooded with ivy, would form a picturesque object if it stood distinct from the habitations in its neighbourhood". The architects of the Gothic Revival were able to exploit this essential characteristic of standing alone in the development of smaller houses standing in their own grounds. In 1774 Payne Knight started building a prototype of many other crenellated villas, with his Downton Castle in Herefordshire, "having at once the advantage of a picturesque object and of an elegant and convenient dwelling".

The crenellated feature of the Gothic Revival can be found not only in some suburban villas but also in three churches in Bath. Between 1814 and 1820 Pinch built St. Mary's, Bathwick, in a Somerset Gothic style, and later in 1829 his son built a similar church at Larkhall. An earlier chapel built in 1765, in the Vineyards, is the Countess of Huntingdon's Chapel which is set back from the terraces of The Paragon. Horace Walpole said in 1766 that the chapel was "very neat, with true Gothic windows..." but added "yet I am not converted". In front of the Chapel is a fine villa for the Countess's

*A picturesque object –
Magdalen Chapel in
Holloway*

own house.   This is far more typical of the scale and treatment of the gothic
villas in the city, in Lyncombe Hill, and the Gothic Cottage in Sion Hill. A
notable group were built in 1828 by Edward Davis, a sometime pupil of
John Soane. The five handsome villas at Entry Hill are irregularly shaped
houses, with crenellated parapets, scattered around a Lyncombe hillside.
They are now surrounded by mature trees in their gardens, but present a
picturesque landscape.

The classical villas built at the same time range from the large mansions
such as 'Vellore' and 'Cranwells' to houses no bigger  than a cottage.
'Vellore', built in about 1830 in Bathwick, was later a school, the Bath
College, then eventually a Nurses' Home. It had extensive and well planted
grounds which included a grotto. 'Cranwells' was built later, in about 1850,
just outside Regency Bath in the suburbs of New Weston.  Its estate of 35
acres was large enough to hold deer and included extensive tree and
shrubbery plantations.   Most of the early nineteenth century suburban
development was of much smaller houses in gardens.  These gardens were
beginning to be a feature of the landscape by 1841, when A.B. Granville
noted:

> *a glance cast in the direction of the south east embraces at once another
> magnificent sweep of succeeding hills, the nearest slopes and knolls of
> which are, ...covered with buildings, principally arranged, however, in this
> case, as detached villas with their surrounding gardens.*

*The classical style of the large mansion -'Vellore' in Bathwick*

Some of these villas were semi-detached or coupled houses. The semi-detached house was not, as Summerson pointed out, a novelty, because examples can be found as far back as 1702 of a pair in Hampstead.

> *The semi-detached house only began its socially successful career after the introduction, probably by Nash, of the unified 'villa' exterior, giving an aesthetic and social consequence of two houses at the price as it were, of one.* (16

It is perhaps ironic that one form of the first semi-detached houses emerged from the 'picturesque' because as well as coupled houses of an irregular form, the ubiquitous semi-detached house with mirrored and symmetrical halves arrived at a time when asymmetry was fashionable. John Pinch was most certainly responsible for the earliest semi-detached houses in Bath, with 1 & 2 Winifred's Dale of 1810, above the earlier terrace of Cavendish Place and below his later Cavendish Crescent. This is a pair of large houses in extensive, bosky grounds. He is, however, also credited with small groups of semi-detached houses at Claremont Place which are dated 1817. Apart (16 from their considerable charm and very careful design, which includes dummy windows in the centre of the composition and curious Soane-like incised lines cut into pilasters, the houses each have small gardens with which most of us are more familiar. With these houses we find for the first time not a rustic or rural landscape brought into the city, but a small garden in urban terms.

The Picturesque Movement emerged from debates on taste which produced a particular form of landscape. As we have seen, this influenced the form of some terraces in the city, producing the dramatic terraces and crescents of Lansdown. The social and economic changes of the beginning of the nineteenth century contributed to the production of smaller houses, villas more ideally suited to the steep and picturesque slopes of Lansdown and Lyncombe. Of these, one type, the semi-detached villa, emerged from the picturesque landscape of Lansdown and in a less sophisticated style was destined to make a significant contribution to the city's landscape a century later. Many of the later nineteenth and twentieth century houses repeated motifs and elements of the Regency period. Of these the gothic style, and in particular the crenellated parapet tower or bay, reappears at various times and in other buildings.

If the Picturesque Movement in Bath can be said to have started with Sham Castle and been established in the suburban villas, it closes with another sham castle. Isambard Brunel used the gothic style for his railway in the Bath area. His Bristol to Bath railway was conceived in 1835 and opened in 1840: The crenellated viaducts and tunnels were essentially picturesque imitation castles. Twerton tunnel appears from the west as a small castle rising from wooded countryside. That these tunnels were awesome there can be no doubt, for Mary Mitford was too frightened at first to go through the Box Tunnel, but she admitted "even the railway [in Bath] contributes by a rare exception to the effect of the landscape". This railway marks the departure of the Regency period and heralds the arrival of the Victorians.

*The arrival of the Victorians – the picturesque railway viaduct – note the lack of trees on Beechen Cliff behind*

*The approach to the beautiful Queen of the West, by the valley of the Avon, is disappointing in the extreme; indeed the slums here are about as bad as those of the Totterdown suburb of Bristol.*

William Black
*Illustrated London News,* 1888

# 8 Victorian Changes

Up until 1836, security and the safety of life and property was of considerable importance in choosing a home. Perhaps this contributed to the attraction of the crenellated villa, which created an illusion of a small, but secure, castle standing in its own grounds. However, with the passing of the Municipal Corporations Act 1835, a re-organised City Corporation set up amongst other measures, one police force, which for the first time could police with the city itself, the former parish of Widcombe and Lyncombe. At the same time, this parish was absorbed with Walcot and Bathwick into the City of Bath. These three parishes had shown a steady growth of their populations during the first third of the nineteenth century and this was not checked until the 1840s, following a severe smallpox epidemic in 1837 and cholera epidemics of 1832, 1848 and 1849. R.S. Neale has shown that the deaths per thousand of population in Bath were second only to the worst in Liverpool, and were particularly severe amongst the working population crowded in the city centre. Edwin Chadwick in his report on the *Sanitary Condition of the Labouring Population of Great Britain* in 1842 quoted Reverend Elwin who collected the relevant statistics for the city. "Whenever we compare one part of Bath with other towns, we find health rising in proportion to the improvement of the residences".

The early Victorian period saw many 'improved residences' built along the main roads, with houses built later in between. The developers of the first suburban villas selected the most attractive and picturesque hillsides of Bathwick, Lyncombe, Lansdown and on the road to Weston. "The Picturesque was 'par excellence' the image of the Victorian suburb" observes Nicholas Taylor. It was anti-aesthetic, a rejection of a collectivised palace front and he said 'Rus in urbe' meant every man possessing his own distinctively composed villa. The most successful suburb was that which afforded the Victorian householder the maximum of privacy and minimum of distraction because, as Donald Olsen has pointed out, the home occupied a central place in any Victorian system of values. Belief in the sanctity of home life was itself a religion, pure and easy to believe. The Victorian middle class tended to turn its back on the rest of society and retreat from the problems and dangers of living in the centre of the city. The suburb provided a healthy environment where home life flourished as nowhere else.

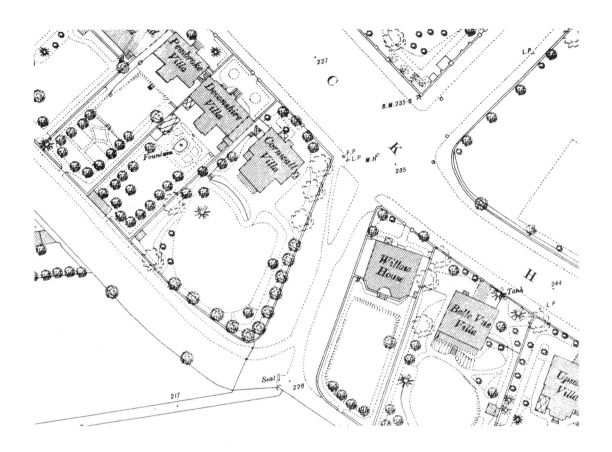

*Gardens of the Bathwick Hill villas as shown on an 1888 Ordnance Survey Map*

Although many of the early suburbs were surrounded by countryside, owners of the new villas created private landscapes with their gardens. New evergreen plants could be used to create the desired privacy behind shrubberies. Many of the villas, particularly in Lansdown and Weston, retain such a landscape and present in the winter months quite large areas of green plants. The 1888 Ordnance Survey plans of the city show in considerable detail the extent of tree and shrub planting in the gardens, including fir or pine trees, greenhouses, and garden seats or fountains. These gardens can be divided into two main groups. Some retain a geometric and Italianate style fashionable in the early Victorian period but others, and particularly later villas such as those in Oldfield Park, tend to have more informal layouts. This more natural approach was being promoted by writers such as William Robinson at the end of the nineteenth century. He was not, however, without his critics who included John Sedding, an Arts and Crafts architect, who was also a founder of the Art Workers Guild. Sedding wrote:

> *To bring nature up to the window of your house, is not only to betray your own deadness to form but to cause a sense of unexpected blankness in the visitor's mind on leaving the well-appointed interior of an English home,*

80

and he continued:

71)

> *as the house is an Art production...there is no code of taste that I know of which would prove that Art is more reprehensible in the garden than in the house.*

*Victoria Nurseries shown on an advertisement in 1850*

The art of the gardener at the beginning of the Victorian period was influenced particularly by the styles developed by Repton. These were promoted by his biographer, Loudon, who in 1838 had coined the term 'Gardenesque' to describe

> *the production of that kind of scenery which is best calculated to display the individual beauty of trees and shrubs and plants in a state of nature; the smoothness of lawns and the smooth surfaces, curved directions, dryness and firmness of gravel walks; in short, it is calculated for displaying the art of the gardener.*

2)

Loudon published a number of books on the subject of domestic gardening and earlier in 1822 founded with his wife *The Gardener's Magazine.* Other magazines followed including in 1841, the newspaper *The Gardener's Chronicle,* in the first issue of which was an advertisement from Salter and Wheeler of Bath's Victoria Nurseries offering new plants, with other advertisements for plants and ingenious equipment to assist in their cultivation. In 1845 duties on glass were removed allowing the more widespread use of greenhouses and conservatories. Loudon had also observed that gardening was being transformed from an art into the sciences of botany and horticulture.

3)

The equipment and greenhouses were essential for the propagation of the new plants that were being brought into this country. Again Loudon offers a comment in his book *The Suburban Gardener and Villa Companion:*

A dreadful Victorian proposal for the front of the Royal Crescent published in 1850 but not realised – thankfully

*No residence in modern style can have a claim to be considered to have been laid out in good taste, in which all the trees and shrubs employed are not either foreign ones or important varieties of indigenous ones.* (17

Victorian gardeners could now draw from a catalogue of a far greater variety of plants than could Pope and his contemporaries. The new plants were being collected for British gardens by traders and explorers at the end of the eighteenth century. By the beginning of Queen Victoria's reign, special expeditions were being undertaken by collectors such as George Vancouver and David Douglas to the North Americas and Archibald Menzies who introduced the monkey puzzle tree from Chile. The plants (17 introduced by these collectors dramatically altered the garden scene by adding evergreens from California, much loved by the Victorians. Miles Hadfield writes:

*How the gardeners of Restoration day would have applauded and welcomed his many additions to their much prized 'greens', and hardy at that.* (17

The gardens of the larger villas were designed to create an overall 'picturesque' effect, but the plants were sited to be seen at their best as individual plants and botanic specimens. A description of Beckford's Tower in 1830 notes that the garden is now planted with thriving woods, shrubs and

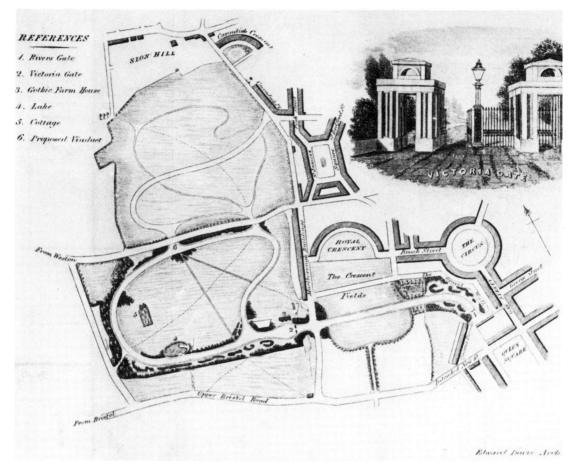

REFERENCES

1. Rivers Gate
2. Victoria Gate
3. Gothic Farm House
4. Lake
5. Cottage
6. Proposed Viaduct

*Edward Davis's layout of 1880 for Victoria Park*

flowers but the garden next to the tower is "of Alpine character, replete with almost every plant and shrub appertaining to such a scheme".

Late Regency improvements in the city paved the way for the introduction of a municipal landscape, for instance Orange Grove, surrounded with railings in 1820. However, the fashions and styles of the Victorian domestic garden could be readily adapted to larger public gardens which were soon to be laid out with displays of bedding out plants and collections of trees. A celebrated print shows a proposal for the area in front of the Royal Crescent laid out with fountains, gravel walks and flower beds. The eighteenth century pleasure gardens developed into the 'municipal park' and several new parks were established in the Victorian city. Although these generally had the advantage over the earlier pleasure gardens in that they were free, Sydney Gardens continued under private management until purchased by the Corporation in 1910.

The earliest and largest of the public open spaces in Bath was land known as High Common and Barton Fields. The latter had been marked on maps from the 1790s as "ground never to be built on". In 1828 it was resolved that High Common should be laid out as a park "affording health

*The gothic farmhouse in Victoria Park*

and recreation to all classes" and was opened as a park in 1830 by the then Princess Victoria. Britton commented at the time:

> *It is intended to be laid out in very picturesque drives, walks, lawns, terraces, plantations, gardens etc. which when effected, will afford a most attractive and delightful place for either healthful exercise or lounging.* (17

The design was indeed delightful and was planned by Davis, who had completed the villas at Entry Hill two years earlier. The healthy exercise could be gained at first only on walks or rides, but no walking was allowed on the grass until very recently. These carriage drives were constructed by William, the son of the eponymous James Macadam, who had been appointed earlier to be the Surveyor of the Bath Turnpike Trust, in 1826. Davis provided a 'picturesque' model farm, and the farmhouse in a cottage orné style remains next to the present nurseries. In 1886 the arboretum in the north west corner of the park was added.

> *The result has been that the park is now confessedly one of the principal features of the city and it has tended not a little to render Bath, what it is now become, a place as well of summer residence as of fashionable winter resort.* (17

## Victorian Changes

Victoria Park was laid out on land which was formerly common land for which there were no plans for development. Following construction of the park, suburban development gradually linked Bath to Weston. It would seem that the foresight of those who brought about the creation of the park was timely because it protected this central area from development.

Whilst the City Council had bought Beechen Cliff in 1860, less foresight was involved in the creation of the next public park. Hedgemead was set out as a park in 1889 on land not available for new building following an earlier disastrous landslide, "by which some hundreds of houses were gradually undermined", wrote Wheatcroft "but as many of these were an eyesore to the neighbourhood on which Hedgemead Park now stands, the loss has been deemed rather a benefit than otherwise". Below Hedgemead much of the meadow land in the Bathwick area had remained undeveloped throughout the nineteenth century, partly as a result of the failure of the City Council to prevent flooding. Earlier, up to 1793, William Pulteney had employed Thomas Telford, the celebrated canal and road engineer, to work on his estates in Bath. Telford reappeared with a partner, James Montague, in the 1820s with proposals to prevent the persistent flooding of the river. These included river works and a new bridge, but the City Corporation was still in debt from earlier improvement works and not able to meet the costs of these plans. They elected instead only to undertake relatively minor works to the old bridge below Beechen Cliff. With the exception of the construction of a few villas, the result was to frustrate various planned developments but as a consequence Bath benefitted from the open spaces that remained.

The gardening and horticultural skills of the Victorians were not only devoted to parks and gardens but began to be applied also to other public spaces. The most notable Victorian designed landscape is perhaps the planned cemeteries. The inadequacies of the existing burial grounds had been identified earlier by the poet, William Wordsworth, who argued in the 'Excursion', for an opportunity for the "soothing influences of nature" to contribute to processes of renovation and decay, although as Keith Thomas has pointed out, there had been in the eighteenth century an association of burial places in gardens. The garden cemetery movement which had begun on the continent soon spread to England when George Carden started the movement in 1824, with the first of many garden cemeteries opening in Liverpool. Wordsworth had quoted his contemporary and fellow poet, John Edwards, who had argued also that existing urban cemeteries were spiritually inadequate. In Bath they were also becoming full

An enabling Act of Parliament allowed land to be bought by parishes outside the city's boundaries for new cemeteries. In 1843 the Abbey parish of St. Peter and St. Paul bought land for a cemetery in Widcombe close to Prior Park which was in a setting described by Dr. Tunstall: "The City of the Dead boasts scenic surroundings of unusual beauty". The 1851 Bath guide describes the grounds as

> *most tastefully laid out under the superintendence of that eminent landscape gardener, the late Mr. Loudon; and the formation of the Abbey cemetery was we believe one of the latest if not the very last effort of his genius and skill.*

85

*Abbey Cemetery laid out by Loudon*

So the ubiquitous Mr. Loudon left in Bath a fitting memorial to his gardening skills in the Abbey Cemetery. Next to this site is the Catholic cemetery with buildings designed by the notable York architect, Charles Hanson, who also designed St. John's Church, South Parade. To the north of the city, Walcot Parish laid out a cemetery below Beckford's Tower. Later other very large cemeteries were laid out for Widcombe and Lyncombe parish on the Lower Bristol Road and for Walcot on the Upper Bristol Road. This last cemetery is most conspicuous from the south of the city and now that its trees have matured, it has created a special landscape of a collection of more 'exotic' species, many of which are evergreen. This extends the Victorian gardening tradition but creates a landscape featuring specimen trees and is very different from the natural landscape of native species.

Had all Victorian suburban development continued with the well-landscaped style of cemeteries, parks and of the Regency villas of Entry Hill, Prior Park Road or of Lansdown and Weston, then the landscape of much of the present city would now be very different. In the middle of the nineteenth century, there was relatively little building and the later suburban development took on a different form. The boom years of the Regency period provided only a shortlived recovery from the depressed state of the city's economy during the Napoleonic Wars. By the mid-1840s the economy slumped again from the bad year of 1837 to a more prolonged state of economic depression. In this time many in the city suffered from

86

36)

37)

38)

starvation and even the elements conspired against a recovery, producing in 1844 and 1845 severe droughts.

The City Corporation was obliged to respond by seeking powers for "more effectively supplying water for the city and several nearby parishes". At the same time, in 1845, the Health of Towns Commission noted that there were no public sewers in the city and the Corporation was urged to put this right. By the 1860s the City Corporation had begun to supply water and start work on various other improvements including the construction of a basic sewerage system. The drought and disease of the 1840s provided a trying time for the City Corporation. The historian, G.M. Young, has pointed out that the end of the decade was also significant for the individual and a turning point in English social history. It was, he suggests, the beginning of the period in which the State intervened to affect people's domestic lives. The first Public Health Acts, the Factory Act of 1847 and the Education Minute of 1846, contributed to a new situation in which an individual was no longer free to help himself. He could not now freely build his own house, dispose of his own sewage, or educate his children. In Bath the combination of piped services and the provisions of building byelaws adopted after the passing of the later Public Health Act of 1875 led to a new form of cheap terraced housing, suitable for an increasing 'working class', finding employment in the growing manufacturing industries of the city.

The 1875 byelaws sought to prevent the construction of housing which would create unhealthy conditions particularly in working class areas. They determined such matters as access, construction, width of streets, and the provision of space and light. By returning to the terrace form of housing, the speculative developer secured considerable advantages in savings on land and costs on the structures. The byelaws did not demand a grid but merely determined the width of the streets. The developer, wishing to provide the most economical distribution of services, produced rows of unrelieved and uniform terraces. Most of the earlier Georgian terraces had been built with a landscaped area or, as cottage-terraces such as Hampton Row, in the countryside. By the end of the nineteenth century the terrace had reappeared in the acceptable if undistinguished form of the suburban or urban terrace grid.

After the provision of capital and land, the next most important factor in determining the provisions of suburban housing is transport and, in particular, access to a place of work. The introduction of public transport services and the development of industries along the river stimulated the development of working class suburbs within walking distance of the new factories and mills. Various industrial businesses had been started in the city centre which had contributed to the increasing squalor of the centre. Here space was limited and the buildings had no greater impact on the landscape than other buildings. However, as firms grew and moved to larger premises along the river, so the opportunity to build larger buildings introduced a new scale and feature in the landscape. The Gas Works and Stothert and Pitt engineering works were soon a significant feature in views across the valley. In the centre of the city, warehouses, maltings and breweries grew up alongside the river with new high buildings which were exceeded in many cases by tall chimneys for the factories' steam power plants. In Twerton a

*Streets of 'Byelaw housing' in South Twerton*

tradition of weaving and brass mills had meant that there were a number of works based round the weirs. New high mills replaced the earlier buildings some of which appear to have been well designed, for Pierce Egan in 1819 states that Mr. Wilkins' broadcloth manufactory was "lofty and capacious, and possesses all the appearance of an elegant mansion".

Egan also observed that Mr. Wilkins had built "...contiguous to his manufactory, a very handsome range of neat and comfortable dwellings built of freestone in the gothic style for his numerous workmen". The growth of the villages of Weston and Twerton was greater than that of any other part of the city at the end of the nineteenth century. Here some villas were built but most of the housing was in the form of terraces. By 1897, Mrs. Wheatcroft, in one of her Picturesque Rambles, conceded that Twerton was no longer picturesque and wrote of "this tremendous suburb, almost

(18

entirely populated by the working class, who are all more or less occupied in ministering to the wants of those on the other side of the water".

The Victorian terraces spread in an undistinguished manner across the slopes in the Lower Oldfield and Twerton areas. By spacing the terraces so that proper ventilation and light were available, modest gardens could be provided at the rear of each house suitable only as a functional space. Stefan Muthesius points out in his analysis of terraced housing that, with so many similar houses in sight of each other, there was no need for a real facade any more. There was, however, some attempt at providing variety in the fronts. Curiously enough, many Bath terraced houses, such as those above Bear Flat, introduced rough rubble stones in the front whilst the back and sides were smooth ashlar. This 'rustic' effect included a very small garden at the front. Unfortunately the terraces allowed no other spaces large enough to provide some relief by tree planting. Larger spaces for recreation were now the responsibility of the Corporation.

Raymond Unwin was to lead a reaction against the philosophy of byelaw housing. He observed in his book *Town Planning in Practice* that whilst the byelaws had done good work in checking the worst evils of overcrowding and bad building, there was no doubt "that the English building byelaws do not work altogether satisfactorily when considered from the point of good architecture".

There was some good suburban domestic architecture built in the Victorian period but it was inevitably in the form of villas for the better off. Here the mature gardens still make a positive contribution to the city's landscape. However, the byelaw housing remains undistinguished albeit very sound. The interpretation of the byelaws left little room for planting and the effect is, in Unwin's words "a dreary monotony of effect which is almost as depressing as it is ugly". The Victorians, however, had established the tradition of the small domestic garden which remains a requirement for most families today. They also introduced municipal controls on building and eventually evolved a municipal landscape of cemeteries and open spaces.

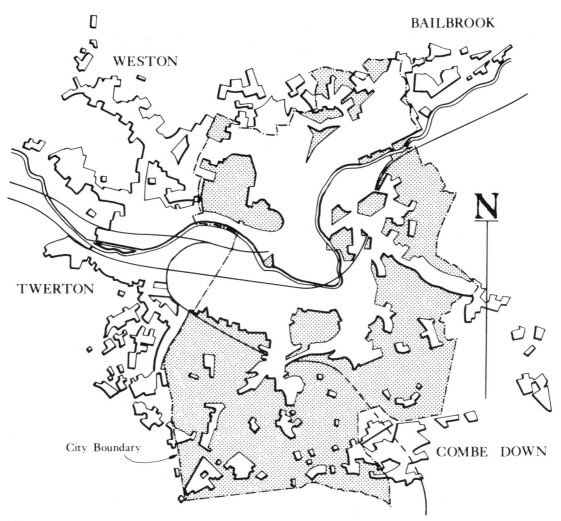

WESTON

BAILBROOK

N

TWERTON

City Boundary

COMBE DOWN

*Twerton not yet part of
the city of 1906*

## 4

*No beauty can arise from the mere aggregation of detached units; there must be something crystalline in the structure, some relationship and grasping of the parts before there can be beauty.*

Raymond Unwin
*City Planning*

# 9   A Planned Landscape

At the end of the nineteenth century the economic fortunes of Bath were slow to pick up and the lack of growth limited the extent of byelaw housing in the city. As it was, much of this suburban development was taking place in neighbouring parishes. Weston and Twerton showed significant growth in the last two decades of the century whilst the population in the city centre showed some decline. Weston remained independent until the 1960s but Twerton was brought into an enlarged city in 1910. Byelaw terraces continued to be built until the First World War but after this, housing took on a new form.

## 5

Although the byelaws would have secured better housing conditions, the 'dreary monotony' effect of the housing was cause for some concern. Raymond Unwin noted in 1909, "it is the lack of beauty, of the amenities of life, more than anything which obliges us to admit that our work of town building in the past century has not been well done". A re-emergence of the gardening and landscape tradition combined with various Victorian Public Health improvement measures, to create a new town planning discipline. In some cities, garden suburbs were developed with low density housing development in the form of 'urban cottages' laid out around open spaces, each house provided with gardens. This inevitable reaction to the monotony of the earlier terraces was given some support with the first Town Planning Act of 1909. This new measure reflected the prevailing belief that suburbanisation was the salvation of the town and all that was necessary was to ensure that the new suburbs were pleasant and healthy. The Act allowed local authorities to prepare town planning schemes for their area. Unwin's achievements of Hampstead Garden Suburb and the development of Letchworth were to dominate the thinking of the emerging town planning profession.

Although no 'garden suburb' was to be built in Bath, Unwin's influence was to extend to some new public housing estates. The wartime Tudor Walters Committee of 1918 which had examined the provision of new working class housing, had been advised by Unwin. He also was retained to prepare a manual of model housing designs. This manual set out the designs and style for several estates which were built on the edge of Bath after the war was over. Unwin had realised that to build an effective number of working class houses, economy was

91

*Bloomfield Crescent on the bare slopes of Odd Down (1824 print)*

essential and this meant they would have to be standardised. He put forward designs for small groups of houses or 'urban cottages' based on his earlier work. The Committee had decided that in order to make the best of the sites for these standardised houses, the schemes should be regulated by town planning principles rather than the earlier byelaws. Although Unwin was an enthusiast for 'picturesque' designs which made the best of existing features of the site, the housing manual had little regard for landscape matters.

Work started in 1920 on the first of the post-war housing estates at Englishcombe Park which was designed by A.J. Taylor. The layout of this estate reflected perhaps to a limited extent the approach pioneered more successfully in garden suburbs elsewhere but this was not to be repeated in the next few undistinguished schemes prepared by the City Engineer, F.P. Sissons. Following a small scheme in the Dolemeads, designs for Rudmore Park were prepared in 1925. These were followed with estates in Larkhall and Southdown Road, but the largest development was to take place at Odd Down in 1930-31. Although the density of this estate was considerably less than earlier byelaw housing, the appearance of the estate remains bleak, relieved only by hedges and a few open spaces. Unwin's advice had been not to build on flat sites because these had no natural features. Regrettably, this had not been heeded, for not only was the site flat, but the area had always lacked tree cover. Richard Warner had in 1800 referred to Bloomfield Crescent impudently exposed on the "bare unwooded side of a lofty hill".

Progress in building 'homes for the heroes' was slow, so that in 1932 under the National Government, the Minister of Health abolished all subsidies on housing except for slum clearance. The task of providing mass housing went back to the speculative developer who was able to take advantage of low interest rates and cheap labour to provide very cheap suburban housing. This produced a further development of the model house designs with the ubiquitous semi-detached house built in its thousands along Britain's arterial roads. Although these houses were very well-built and offered value for money, their developers made less attempt to provide amenities than the local authority housing of a decade earlier. This housing was all speculative and generally all for sale and freehold. Each was provided with a garden and sometimes a garage, but there was no attempt to provide an overall design or any features to relieve the monotony. The layout of the roads was restricted with widths designed to permit adequate sunlight reaching across the road to a living room. The result was no building higher than two storeys.

In due course, the Restriction of Ribbon Development Act 1935 was passed to control the impact of such development. However, before this in 1929, the City and County of Bristol with the Bath County Borough and surrounding local authorities invited Patrick Abercrombie and B.F. Brueton to prepare in outline a Regional Plan. Their report, published in 1930, was an enlightened piece of work which looked at opportunities for growth in the region. In their report they examined, amongst other things, the problems of suburban and ribbon development. It is especially

*Homes for Heroes built at Englishcombe Park in the 1930s*

93

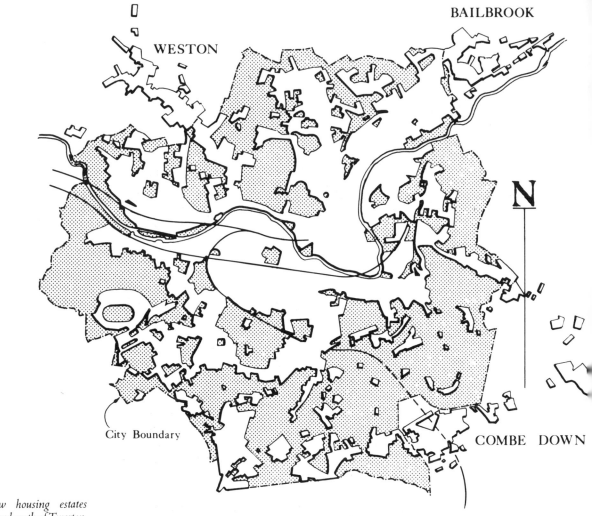

WESTON

BAILBROOK

N

City Boundary

COMBE DOWN

*New housing estates extend south of Twerton, 1936*

significant in that, for the first time, the landscape of the area was assessed and recommendations put forward to "conserve the existing landscape character and also preventing straggling development".

(19

As might be expected, the landscape of the area around Bath came in for special attention:

*It is no exaggeration to say that the attraction of Bath consists no more in the compact urbanity of the town than in the romantic beauty of its irregular coombes and hills so far largely unspoiled.*

(20

In the Report, Abercrombie and Brueton recommended a special landscape zoning in which residential development would be restricted and amenities safeguarded. "Bath is shown as a compact city in a setting of beautiful country specially to be preserved". This prototype Green Belt

(20

A SMALL NEIGHBOURHOOD UNIT SHOPPING CENTRE

*Clean spacious architecture proposed in the 'Plan for Bath'*

was based as much on an assessment of landscape character as on the desire to restrict the coalition of towns and cities which was the justification for the statutory Green Belts of the 1950s and 1960s. The Green Belt measures were soon to be incorporated into the Bath and District Planning Scheme which was inaugurated in 1933. By July 1939 much of the land around the city had been covered by voluntary agreements to protect the Green Belt, as well as designated woodlands, trees and streams.

Patrick Abercrombie had an opportunity to develop further the concept of the Green Belt when he returned to prepare a plan for the reconstruction of the city, following the wartime bombing. His *Plan for Bath*, which he prepared with the City Engineer and Planning Officer, did more than consider the bomb-damaged sites. For the first time it provided a plan for the development of the whole city. In this, the concept of the Green Belt was fundamental to the character of the city and its landscape, because it directed new suburban development largely within the boundary of the city. Some development, however, was proposed for Weston and Combe Down which at that time were still outside the city.

The immediate post-war years were a time of austerity and many difficulties, but they were also a time of hope. The architects who were commissioned to build the new housing sought to build a new society and a better Britain. They believed that this was in part going to be achieved by providing better living conditions in the new housing. In this they were guided by a new manual, the 1944 Housing Manual, which had been influenced by the Ministry of Health. Although a new Ministry of Housing was co-ordinating the rebuilding programme, health considerations were of importance with requirements for space and light.

The rationing of building material restricted all but a few private building initiatives. Schemes for new housing in Bath were, to begin with, built by the City Corporation. The *Plan for Bath* put forward sketches of new suburbs built around open spaces, neighbourhood shopping centres or community centres. The first houses to be put up were prefabricated units, the 'prefabs', providing as many new homes as possible, but

95

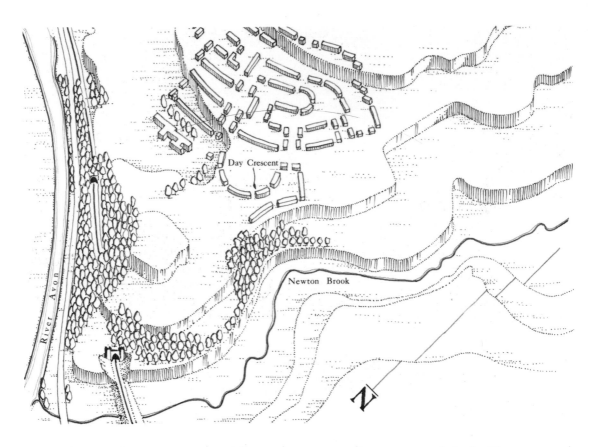

Day Crescent

Newton Brook

River Avon

*Post-war housing making the best of a superb site in the 1940s* more permanent homes were soon to be constructed. In the Plan, proposals for the developments above Twerton were illustrated with outlines for other estates such as Moorlands and parts of Weston.

These designs and Abercrombie's Plan show a development of Unwin's Garden Suburb ideas and, perhaps, reflect the eighteenth century concept of the 'picturesque' model village. One of the most notable of the schemes built immediately after the war is Day Crescent. Shown in the *Plan for Bath,* it was conceived while the war still being fought. The scheme makes the best use of the contours of the site overlooking the Pennyquick valley. The houses are prefabricated, semi-detached, Cornish units laid out in a crescent. It should not be compared with its more illustrious predecessors, the Royal Crescent or Lansdown Crescent, but with Unwin's housing in Letchworth or Hampstead. Here the scheme does everything it was attempting to do by creating an up-to-date picturesque development. The authors of the *Plan for Bath* were familiar with Unwin's work and effectively repeat his advice. They say in the report:

> *There is more in housing estate design than the mere building of pairs of semi-detached villas along the estate roads. More attention should be paid to grouping of buildings and the placing of open spaces; advantage should be taken of the natural features of the sites, the siting and arboreal treatment of the roads could with advantage receive greater consideration.*

In Day Crescent we see the roads tucked away behind the houses whose *Blaise Hamlet creates a* scale and arrangement around the communal green are similar to the *picturesque village en-* character of Blaise Hamlet and thereby show its origin to be in the *closure* 'picturesque village' movement. Curiously Abercrombie's advice on the provision of gardens was to discourage fences and walls. This reflects the experience of Blaise Hamlet where houses are sited within a green space. However, the lack of the definition of a garden has deteriorated in recent housing development to become featureless and criticised as 'prairie planting' or a 'ranch style'.

Once traditional materials became more readily available, new terraces were soon to be built on other housing estates. The Moorlands estate was a winning design in a housing competition in 1946. Here traditional housing construction was brought back to provide new local authority homes laid out with large areas of open space. This development of enormous charm is no longer a reborn 'picturesque village' but one which created its own wide open landscape. Here the spaces and houses were designed together and carefully related. Hedges and walls were abandoned in line with the recommendations of Abercrombie who advised against all but low front walls. With hindsight, the delicate planting of trees such as silver birches has not provided a park-like landscape contributing to the overall landscape of the city in the same way as the Royal Victoria Park. To some extent this is an unfair criticism because the slopes of Odd Down and Southdown never had many trees to begin with. The maps of 1888 show

N

City Boundary

*Much of the undeveloped land around Bath in 1980 is protected by the Green Belt*

very few trees, limited to hedgerows, whereas the Lansdown area is relatively well-treed in hedges and small fields and paddocks. With land for new housing becoming scarce in Bath, the wide verges and other spaces appear to be a poor use of land and would clearly come under pressure to be released for new development. They were, however, carefully designed as part of the development with the intention of providing a community with healthy living conditions as well as creating a 'picturesque' effect.

The public housing schemes built immediately after the war, provided a brief renaissance for the picturesque or 'designed' landscape. It proved to be too brief, for in spite of the laudable social objectives of the architects and the Ministry of Housing, a new objective was given precedence. A new government administration took office after the general election of 1952 which promoted a building programme concentrating on quantity at the expense of quality. Controls on building were removed and the private sector was encouraged to build again. From the mid-1950s the nature of building was to change and with it the character of many parts of the city. Some new housing was built on sites cleared by bomb damage or as a result of slum clearance for public health reasons. However, much more housing was built on the edges of the city and on infill sites.

New housing schemes were built at higher densities and these created fewer opportunities for open spaces. Unlike the Day Crescent and Moorlands estates which were built around an open space so that the landscape was an integral part of the design, the newer plans sought to achieve primarily a density, or later a 'cost yardstick', so that landscape considerations were left on one side. Very rarely in the last thirty years has landscape been put forward as an essential part of the concept of a design. This situation has not been helped by the post-war planning system. This was established by the Town and Country Planning Act 1947 and reinforced with successive Acts. The system which requires planning permision to be granted for most development also allows the permission to be granted subject to conditions. These conditions usually require details to be prepared later and inevitably the details include landscape matters. The system has reinforced a neglect of designed landscapes in the years following the Second World War.

The present approach to architecture and planning does not compare favourably with the various movements of the eighteenth and early nineteenth centuries in terms of creating a designed landscape. There was a brief revival of the 'picturesque' approach in the garden suburb and new housing built immediately after the war but the results of this were not enough to make a significant contribution to the landscape of the city. The twentieth century has, however, seen two 'movements' become established and each in their was has affected, and will continue to affect the city's landscape. A Green Belt movement produced early results at Bath where a green belt had been set around the city for nearly fifty years. This device, which is intended to contain the growth of the city, is as important as the great landscaped parks of Brown and Repton. Up till now Green Belts have been regarded as a defensive zone set up to prevent the sprawling growth of the city, but they do create a countryside landscape protected from development around and into the city.

The second movement is the Town and Country Planning movement. This has established a system to control the worst excesses of development, determine the ordered use of land, and guide investment to where it is needed. How successful this will be in protecting the 'landscape' that has survived from the past, we shall have to wait and see. Whether it can create or stimulate an appropriate new landscape for Bath remains to be seen. Will the planning system be equal to the task ? It is a big task.

*Ornamental gardening
at its best, in Prior Park*

*Ornamental gardening, which in ... countries of the European continent, constitutes a part of the architect's profession; is here in other hands: and, with a few exceptions, in very improper ones...*

William Chambers
*On Civil Architecture,* 1791

# 10 The Pleasing Art

William Chambers, in his treatise *On Civil Architecture,* took the view that should the 'pleasing art' of gardening be practised by men trained in the study of composition, then we should expect to find a greater variety of landscape gardening, and "a far higher perfection in works of that sort than now can be expected". The people expected to produce this higher standard of gardening were architects, who in their time would probably have travelled on the Grand Tour or at least would have been familiar with a variety of classical buildings and places. The various eighteenth century architectural styles in Bath show that its architects reflected in their schemes the then current fashions in landscape design in various ways. John Wood the elder was clearly an able and practical landscape gardener and his designs for Queen Square are 'palaces' around a formal parterre.

The arrangement of the Circus is probably derived from his experience of ronds-points in landscape gardens. His son's Royal Crescent reflects the later fashionable 'Brownian' landscape of a country house rising from the turf of a parkland setting. The Lansdown crescents and villas of the end of the eighteenth century were designed to create a picturesque effect, not only in the setting of the building, but also in the creation of a wider landscape of a particular romantic style. Finally, the Romantic movement produced the 'picturesque' villa which eventually evolved into the Regency and Victorian suburban house. These buildings were all products of a particularly close relationship between the architecture of the building and its landscape setting. All have contributed to the overall landscape of the city and each identifiable period of the city's growth has distinct character. The picturesque terraces for the most part retain their bosky background and the villa landscape provides an area of varied and mature trees around the centre of the city.

The principal change in attitudes to the landscape might be related to a significant change in society that occurred in the middle of the nineteenth century. Up to the 1840s an individual was free from many controls. With the passing of the first of the Public Health Acts, and Factory Acts of 1845, control by the state began to be introduced, leaving less freedom for a property owner. This has been further compounded by the Town and Country Planning Act of 1947 which introduced yet more restrictions on development. It is perhaps unfortunate that this universal system tended to relegate aesthetic considerations in favour of land use controls. Landscape matters have become very often of secondary importance.

We could be forgiven for dismissing current architectural practice, because it does not provide with each new development a positive contribution to a future landscape for the city. Architects of many new buildings seem to treat the sites as pieces of land conveniently available for development. Few new developments respect the character of the site and as a consequence fit uncomfortably on it. The cupidity of the development market results more often than not in the over-development of the site, too many buildings on too small a space and as a result, a mediocre scrap of land left around the edge which is then 'landscaped' as an afterthought.

Here the word 'landscaped' is used in a way which is quite different from the 'landscaping work' of the eighteenth century builders and architects. It would seem that the authors responsible for some new developments may only think about the left over space once the basic design and costs of the building have been worked out and not as a starting point of the design. Alternatively a tree is squeezed in on a bit of remaining land, because it might help the scheme to get planning permission. Perhaps also the use of conditions to planning permission, whereby permission has been granted subject to landscaping work being completed later, has further relegated 'landscape'. This lack of awareness of the need to design the whole site is highlighted by the invention of a rubber stamp depicting a plan or elevation of a tree. With this useful tool, an architect or other designer of a scheme, does not have to draw a tree on the plan but can just stamp it on once or twice or even create a whole forest!

As I mentioned in the first chapter, the word 'landscape' is a painter's word introduced from the Dutch in the sixteenth century as 'landskip', to describe a pictorial representation of countryside. It is only now that the word has taken on other meanings, firstly, to include the sense of the countryside represented in a picture, more loosely a sketch of countryside as a visual phenomenon, and secondly as a term for those site works which are usually gardening or tree planting around a building. John Barrell has pointed out that there is no word in English for a tract of land, of whatever extent, which is apprehended visually, but not necessarily pictorially, and suggests the nearest is probably terrain. If our language can (21( give clues to the state of our society or culture, then the very lack of words to describe 'landscape' suggests an inability to discuss or think about what we are seeing or want to see. It may be, however, that now we are more reluctant to discuss the landscape of the city. In the eighteenth century Pope, Walpole and Gilpin were instrumental in determining taste with their poems and prose. Kenneth Clark even suggests that their literature influenced architecture, particularly that of the Gothic Revival and the (21 'picturesque' landscape. It can hardly be claimed that present literature or its equivalent, the television, is influencing landscape design.

The character of our city is made up of its buildings and its surrounding trees and gardens. So much of this is now taken for granted, that the gradual decay or decline of the treed or green parts of the city is occurring without a clear indication or agreement of what is wanted to take its place. There are frequent and well-publicised attempts to protect various well-loved open spaces from development. Usually, however, the need for new houses takes precedence over an amenity or a view. This is in part due to the fact that it is easier and more convenient to measure housing need by numbers of people without homes and the possible number of buildings that can be fitted on a piece of land. It is not so easy to measure the quality of a landscape and we may not even have the right words to do so. Trying to define 'amenity' has been likened to defining an elephant, which is difficult to describe, but is possible to recognise when we see it. It is possible to recognise in Bath's landscape that here is something that is precious, but defining what is valuable still eludes us.

Unlike buildings, which are relatively permanent if they are well maintained, trees and gardens are more like us - they decay and then die. Like us, they are susceptible to changing fashions; an eighteenth century garden valued once as a place within which young bucks of the day could perambulate and be seen, today no longer has that role. We tend now not to perambulate and young bucks are more interested in their bikes. Should the garden be retained as an historical memento or as a complement to the surrounding historic buildings ? Should it be kept as a copy of a formal parterre or should it be laid out as an open space more in keeping with today's needs ? It is significant that whilst the owner of an historic building is encouraged with grants, or required by law, to retain the character of his building, there is no such compunction on him to maintain his garden in any particular style. Window sashes are faithfully copied to repeat the eighteenth century originals, but so far, the owner can design a garden in any way, and with plants that arrived in this country a century later. There is now an emerging science or profession of landscape gardeners, expert in historic landscapes and gardens. It may be that they will be able to restore these gardens to demonstrate what they were once like and to maintain them to complement the adjacent historic house. This will open up the debate of whether all open spaces should be restored to their original condition: for instance, should the centre of the Circus be once more paved, as first laid out, or retain its grass ?

It may be argued that in the same way that historic buildings have been protected and conserved, it should be a public duty to protect and conserve the surviving historic landscape. Years ago, whilst some houses and monuments had been identified as historic, the owners still had the right to knock them down or do what they liked with them. It has taken some fifty years in Bath to change opinion so that it is accepted that the conservation of buildings is a duty. In this respect, today's society is a custodian or a steward looking after these buildings for the future. Should it be charged with the same task for Bath's historic landscape ? The answer must be yes, but it cannot wait fifty years to be accepted because within that time much of the landscape cover will have disappeared. The protection of a landscape, which is a living thing, is not just a matter of preventing any more development. Capability Brown, Repton or the designers of the crescents in Lansdown would certainly not have agreed with that. They believed that their buildings improved the landscape. So too could new development, but only when its architects are able to design buildings in a way which makes a positive contribution to the overall character of the city, either in terms of a street scene or when viewed from across the valley. To be able better to achieve this, architects and the people of Bath should understand why the character is what it is and how it has been created.

Pevsner, in one of his Reith lectures in 1955, argued that we are in need of a policy of healthy, attractive urban planning. There is, he said,

> *an English national planning theory in existence which need only be recognised and developed. It is hidden in the writings of the improvers from Pope to Uvedale Price and Payne Knight.* (212

In 1751, Pope had urged Lord Burlington to "let Nature never be forgot. Consult the Genius of the Place itself". Here Pope referred to the *genius loci*, (21: a mythological spirit of the place as recorded in Virgil's *Aeneid*, but taken (21 over and given a new meaning. Pevsner concludes:

> *The 'genius loci', if we put it in modern planning terms, is the character of the site, and the character of the site is, in a town, not only the geographical but also the historical, social, and especially aesthetic character.* (21

By looking at the growth of Bath in terms of its landscape, we may be able to see and understand more clearly, the character of various parts of the city and hopefully define and agree the value we should place on the city's landscape, the Genius of Bath.

> *Great Nature scorns control...*
> *Yet she permits thy art, discreetly us'd,*
> *To smooth or scoop the rugged and the plain,*
> *But done with caution; else expect, bold man,*
> *The injured Genius of the place to rise*
> *In self defence, and like some fiend*
> *That frowns in Gothic story, swift destroy*
> *By night, the puny labours of thy day.*

William Mason,
*English Garden,* 1778

# Bibliography

I have referred to, or quoted from, the works listed in the bibliography. There are, however, a few which are essential reading and provide a background to this account of Bath's landscape. Essential for any study of buildings in Bath are Mowbray Green's classic work *The Eighteenth Century Architecture of Bath,* Walter Ison's *The Georgian Buildings of Bath*, and Sir Nikolaus Pevsner's ubiquitous *Buildings of England – North Somerset and Bristol.* The most thorough work on architectural history, Sir John Summerson's *Architecture in Britain 1530-1830*, provides a background on the history of architectural design. Whilst there are many books describing the architecture of Bath, there are surprisingly, not many setting out the growth of the city. Bryan Little's ever delightful *The Building of Bath* examines the architecture of Bath with a very readable account of the growth of the city, and John Haddon's book *Bath* brings the history more or less up to date. A more scholarly examination of the growth of the city is set out in R.S. Neale's *Bath – A Social History 1680-1850*.

There is no account of landscape in Bath, but W.G. Hoskin's *Making of the English Landscape* provides a very readable general account of the history of landscape. For a background to landscape gardening, Miles Hadfield's classic work *A History of British Gardening* is indispensable, and the *Genius of the Place* by John Dixon Hunt and Peter Willis contains many original texts. The changing attitudes of our predecessors to landscape and nature have been thoroughly examined and set out by Keith Thomas in *Man and the Natural World.* There are, however, two books which above all focus on landscape matters and provide part of the theme for the conclusions to my account of the use of landscape in Bath; these are John Barrell's *The Idea of Landscape and the Sense of Place 1730-1848* and Sir Nikolaus Pevsner's masterpiece, *The Englishness of English Art*.

NOTE: The editions to which I have referred are those cited last below.

anon. — *Bath Guide,* Bath, 1851

anon. — 'A Description of the Seat of Ralph Allen Esq. Near the City of Bath', *The Universal Magazine,* May 1754

anon. — *Historical and Local New Bath Guide,* John Browne, Bath, 1802

ABERCROMBIE, PATRICK & BRUETON, B.F. — *Bath and Bristol Regional Planning Scheme,* London, 1930

ABERCROMBIE, PATRICK ET AL. — *A Plan for Bath,* Bath, 1945

ACKERMAN, JAMES — *Palladio,* Penguin Books, Harmondsworth, 1966, (1981 edn.)

ANSTEY, CHRISTOPHER — *New Bath Guide,* Bath, 1830/2 edn.

ASHWORTH, WILLIAM — *The Genesis of Modern British Planning,* Routledge and Kegan Paul, London 1954 (1968 edn.)

ASTON, MICHAEL — *Interpreting the Landscape,* B.T. Batsford, London, 1985

ATKYNS, SIR ROBERT — *Ancient and Present State of Glostershire,* 2nd edn. London, 1712.

AUSTEN, JANE — *Northanger Abbey,* London, 1818; Penguin Books, Harmondsworth, 1972 (1975 edn.)

BARRELL, JOHN — *The Idea of Landscape and the Sense of Place 1730-1848,* Cambridge U.P., Cambridge, 1972

BARRON, R.S. — *The Geology of Wiltshire,* Moonraker Press, Bradford-on-Avon, 1976

BATH CITY COUNCIL — *Forty Years On,* Bath City Council, Bath 1985

BLACK, WILLIAM — 'Strange Adventures of a Town Boat', *Illustrated London News,* 26th May, 9th June, 16th June 1888

BRITTON, JOHN — 'Preface' to Anstey (op.cit.)

BROWN, JANE — *The Everywhere Landscape,* Wildwood House, London, 1982

BURKE, EDMUND — *A Philosophical Enquiry into the Origin of our Ideas of the Sublime and the Beautiful,* 1756

CARTER, TOM — *The Victorian Garden,* Bell and Hyman, London, 1984

CHALKIN, C.W. — *The Provincial Towns of Georgian England,* Edward Arnold, London, 1974

CHAMBERS, WILLIAM — *On Civil Architecture,* 1791 1825 edn. quoted in Eliot and Stern, op.cit.)

CHANDLER, MARY — *A Description of Bath, A Poem,* London, 1734

CLARK, SIR KENNETH — *Civilisation,* John Murray and BBC Books, London 1969

CLARK, SIR KENNETH — *Gothic Revival,* John Murray, London, 1928; Penguin Books, Harmondswoth, 1962

COLLINSON, REV. JOHN — *The History and Antiquities of the County of Somerset,* R. Cruttwell, Bath, 1791

COOK, OLIVE — *The English House through Seven Centuries,* Thomas Nelson, 1968; Penguin Books, Harmondsworth, 1984

CRAWFORD, PETER — *The Living Isles,* BBC Books, London, 1985

CRESSWELL, PAUL — *Bath in Quotes,* Ashgrove Press, Bath, 1985

CRUIKSHANK, DAN — *Georgian Buildings,* Weidenfield and Nicolson, London, 1985

CUNLIFFE, BARRY — *Roman Bath Discovered,* Routledge and Kegan Paul, London 1971

CURL, JAMES STEVENS — 'The Architecture and Planning of the Nineteenth Century Cemeteries', *Journal of the Garden History Soc.,* Summer 1975, Vol. III, No. 3

CURL, JAMES STEVENS — *A Celebration of Death,* Constable, London, 1980

DARLEY, GILLIAN — *Villages of Vision,* Architectural Press, London, 1975; Paladin Books, London, 1978

DE LA BECHE, HENRY — *Report on the City of Bath and its Sanitary Condition,* 1845

DEFOE, DANIEL — *A Tour through the Whole Island of Great Britain,* London 1724-7; Penguin Books, Harmondsworth, 1971

DOBBIE, BEATRICE — *An English Rural Community – Batheaston with St. Catherine,* Bath University Press, Bath, 1969

DUKE, KATY — 'Garden Buildings of Prior Park', unpublished thesis, University of Bath, 1982

EDWARDS, ARTHUR — *The Design of Suburbia,* Pembridge Press, London, 1981

EGAN, PIERCE — *Walks Through Bath,* Mary Meyler and Son, Bath, 1819

ELIOT, SIMON & STERN, BEVERLEY (eds.) — *The Age of Enlightenment,* Ward Lock Educational/Open University, London,1979

ESHER, LIONEL — *A Broken Wave,* Allen Lane, Harmondsworth, 1981

EVELYN, JOHN — *The Diary of John Evelyn,* William Bray, London, 1818; Oxford U.P., Oxford, 1985

FIELDING, HENRY — *Tom Jones,* Andrew Miller, London, 1749; Penguin Books, Harmondsworth 1966 (1973 edn.)

FIENNES, CELIA — *Journeys 1685 and 1703,* Macdonald, London, 1982, Futura, London, 1983

FINBERG, H.P.R. — 'Roman and Saxon Withington – A Study in Continuity', Department of Local History, Leicester University, Occasional Paper No. 8 (quote in Aston, op.cit.)

FLEMING, LAWRENCE & GORE, ALAN — *The English Garden,* Michael Joseph, London, 1980

GADD, DAVID — *Georgian Summer – Bath in the Eighteenth Century,* Moonraker Press, Bradford-on-Avon, 1971 (1977 edn.)

GRANVILLE, A.B. — *The Spas of England and Principal Bathing Places,* Henry Colburn, London, 1841

GREEN, MOWBRAY — *The Eighteenth Century Architecture of Bath,* George Gregory, Bath, 1904

GRIGSON, GEOFFREY — *Shell Country Alphabet,* Michael Joseph, London, 1966

HADDON, JOHN — *Bath,* B.T. Batsford, London, 1973

HADFIELD, MILES — *A History of British Gardening,* Hutchinson, London, 1960; Penguin Books, Harmondsworth, 1985

HAMPSON, NORMAN — *The Enlightenment,* Penguin Books, Harmondsworth, 1968 (1976 edn.)

HAVINDEN, MICHAEL — *The Somerset Landscape,* Hodder and Stoughton, London, 1981

HOGARTH, WILLIAM — *The Analysis of Beauty,* 1753 (quoted in Eliot and Stern, op.cit.)

HOSKINS, W.G. — *The Making of the English Landscape,* Hodder and Stoughton, London, 1955; Penguin Books, Harmondsworth, 1970

HUMPHREYS, A.R. — 'Architecture and Landscape' in the *Pelican Guide to English Literature,* Part 4, (ed. Boris Ford), Penguin Books, Harmondsworth, 1957 (1973 edn.)

HUNT, JOHN DIXON & WILLIS, PETER (eds.) — *The Genius of the Place – the English Landscape Garden 1620-1820,* Paul Elek, London, 1975

IBBETSON, J.C., LAPORTE, J. & HASSELL, J. — *A Picturesque Guide to Bath, Bristol Hotwells, the River Avon, and Adjacent Country,* Hookham and Carpenter, London, 1793

ISON, WALTER — *The Georgian Buildings of Bath,* Faber and Faber, London, 1948; 2nd ed. Kingsmead Press, Bath, 1980

JACKSON, FRANK — *Sir Raymond Unwin,* A.Zwemmer, London, 1985

JONES, RICHARD — 'Life of Richard Jones', unpublished manuscript, 1858

KING, AUSTIN J. — 'The Monks of Bath in the 13th and 14th Centuries', Bath Literary and Philosophical Association, Bath, 1895

KNIGHT, RICHARD PAYNE — *The Landscape, a Didactic Poem,* 1795

KNIGHT, RICHARD PAYNE — *An Analytical Inquiry into the Principles of Taste,* 1808

LEES-MILNE, JAMES — *The Age of Adam,* B.T. Batsford, London, 1947

LELAND, JOHN — *Itinerary,* 1711-12; ed. Lucy Toulmin Smith, London, 1906-10

LITTLE, BRYAN — *The Building of Bath,* Collins, London, 1947

LITTLE, BRYAN — *Prior Park – Its History and Description,* Prior Park College, Bath, 1975

LOUDON, J.C. — *An Encyclopaedia of Cottage Farm and Villa Architecture and Furniture,* London 1833

LOUDON, J.C. — *The Suburban Gardener and Villa Companion,* London, 1838

MAINWARING, ROWLAND — *Annals of Bath,* Mary Meyler and Son, Bath, 1838

MALINS, EDWARD — *English Landscaping and Literature 1660-1840,* Oxford U.P., Oxford, 1966

MASON, WILLIAM — *The English Garden,* London, 1772-81

MILTON, JOHN — *Paradise Lost,* 1667

MITCHELL, ANTHONY — 'Park and Garden at Dyrham' in the *National Trust Yearbook 1977,* National Trust, London, 1977

MITFORD, MARY RUSSELL — *Recollections of a Literary Life,* London, 1851

MOORE, JOHN — 'Medieval Forest of Kingswood', in *Avon Past* No. 7, Autumn 1982

MURRAY, PETER — *Architecture of the Italian Renaissance,* B.T. Batsford, London, 1963

MUTHESIUS, STEFAN — *The English Terraced House,* Yale U.P., London, 1982

NEALE, R.S. — *Bath – A Social History 1680-1850,* Routledge and Kegan Paul, London, 1981

OLSEN, DONALD J. — *The Growth of Victorian London,* B.T. Batsford, London, 1976; Penguin Books, Harmondsworth, 1979

PAGE, WILLIAM (ed.) — *The Victoria County History of Somerset,* Constable, London, 1911

PENNY, N.B. — 'Commercial Garden Necropolis of the early nineteenth century and its critics', *Journal of the Garden History Society,* Summer 1974, Vol.II, No.3

PEVSNER, SIR NIKOLAUS — *An Outline of European Architecture*, Penguin Books, Harmondsworth, 1943 (1963 edn.)

PEVSNER, SIR NIKOLAUS — *The Englishness of English Art,* Architectural Press, London, 1956; Penguin Books, Harmondsworth, 1964

PEVSNER, SIR NIKOLAUS — *Buildings of England – North Somerset and Bristol,* Penguin Books, Harmondsworth, 1958

POCOCKE, DR. RICHARD — *The Travels through England,* 1754, Camden Society, 1889

POPE, ALEXANDER — 'Essay from the Guardian', 1713, (quoted in Hunt and Willis, op. cit.)

POPE, ALEXANDER — 'Epistle IV to Richard Boyle, Earl of Burlington, on the use of Riches', 1731 (quoted in Hunt and Willis, op.cit.)

RACKHAM, OLIVER — *Trees and Woodland in the British Landscape,* J.M. Dent, London, 1976 (1983 edn.)

REED, MICHAEL — *The Georgian Triumph, 1700-1830,* Routledge and Kegan Paul, London, 1983; Paladin Books, London, 1984

REPTON, HUMPHREY — *Fragments on the Theory and Practice of Landscape Gardening,* 1816

RICHARDSON, SAMUEL — *The History of Sir Charles Grandison,* 1753-4 (quoted in Hunt and Willis, op.cit.)

ROLT, L.T.C. — *Thomas Telford,* Longman, Harlow, 1958; Penguin Books, Harmondsworth, 1985

RYKWERT, J. & A. — *The Brothers Adam,* Collins, London, 1985

SCOTT, MAURICE — *Discovering Widcombe and Lyncombe,* Maurice Scott, Bath, 1984

SEDDING, JOHN — *Garden Craft Old and New,* Kegan Paul, Trench, Trubner, London, 1891 (quoted in Carter, op.cit.)

SHARP, THOMAS — *Town Planning,* Penguin Books, Harmondsworth, 1940

SITWELL, SACHEVERELL — *British Architecture and Craftsmen,* B.T. Batsford, London, 1945; Pan Books, London, 1960

SMITH, R.A.L. — *Bath,* B.T. Batsford, London, 1944

SOUTHEY, ROBERT — *Letters from England,* 1807; ed. Jack Simmons, Alan Sutton, Gloucester, 1984

STROUD, DOROTHY — *Capability Brown,* Faber and Faber, London 1975

SUMMERSON, SIR JOHN — *Heavenly Mansions,* W.W. Norton, London 1949 (1963 edn.)

SUMMERSON, SIR JOHN — *Architecture in Britain, 1530-1830,* Penguin Books, Harmondsworth, 1953

SUMMERSON, SIR JOHN — *The Life and Work of John Nash, Architect,* Allen and Unwin, London, 1980

SWITZER, STEPHEN — *Ichnographia Rustica,* 1718 (quoted in Hunt and Willis, and Mitchell, opera cit.)

| | |
|---|---|
| SYDENHAM, SYDNEY | *Bath Pleasure Gardens of the 18th Century Using Metal Tickets,* 1907; Kingsmead Press, Bath, 1969 |
| TAYLOR, NICHOLAS | *The Village in the City,* Maurice Temple Smith, London 1973 |
| TAYLOR, NICHOLAS | 'The Awful Sublimity of the City', in Dyos and Wolff, *The Victorian City,* Vol.I, Routledge and Kegan Paul, London, 1973 |
| TEMPLE, NIGEL | *John Nash and the Village Picturesque,* Alan Sutton, Gloucester, 1979 |
| THOMAS, KEITH | *Man and the Natural World,* Allen Lane, Harmondsworth, 1983; Penguin Books, Harmondsworth, 1984 |
| TUNSTALL, DR. JAMES | *Rambles about Bath,* R.E. Peach, Bath, 1847 (1889 edn.) |
| UNWIN, RAYMOND | *Town Planning in Practice,* T. Fisher Unwin, London, 1909 (1919 edn.) |
| UNWIN, RAYMOND | 'City Planning' (quoted in Jackson, op.cit.) |
| WALPOLE, HORACE | *Journals of Visits to Country Seats,* Walpole Society, Vol.16, 1927 |
| WARD, NED | *A Step to the Bath,* London 1700 (quoted in Cresswell, op.cit.) |
| WARNER, REV. RICHARD | *A Walk through some of the Western Counties of England,* G.G. and J. Robinson, London, 1800 |
| WATTS, WILLIAM | *Select Views of the Principal Buildings and other interesting and picturesque objects in the cities of Bath and Bristol and their environs,* London, 1819 |
| WHEATCROFT, LOUISE | 'Picturesque Village Rambles Around Bath', *The Bath and County Graphic,* Bath, 1897 |
| WITTKOWER, RUDOLF | *Palladio and English Palladianism,* Thames and Hudson, London, 1974 (1983 edn.) |
| WOOD, JOHN | *A Description of Bath,* W. Bathoe and T. Lownds, London, 1765; Kingsmead Press, Bath, 1969 |
| YOUNG, G.M. | *Portrait of an Age – Victorian England,* Oxford U.P., Oxford, 1934 (1977 edn.) |

## BIBLIOGRAPHICAL REFERENCES

1 Austen J., 1818 (1975 edn.), p.125
2 Austen J., 1818 (1975 edn.), p.125
3 Repton (quoted by Hunt and Willis 1975, p.372)
4 Austen H., 1818 (1975 edn.), p.33
5 Ibbetson et al, 1793, p.103
6 Egan, 1819, p.242
7 Black, 1888, p.571
8 Mitford, 1851, p.292
9 Egan, 1819, p.268
10 Wheatcroft, 1897, p.36
11 Smith, 1944, p.91
12 Evelyn, 1706 (1985 edn.), p.47
13 Pevsner, 1958, p.90
14 Leland (ed. Toulmin-Smith 1910), Vol.I, pp.139-140
15 Fiennes, (1983 edn.) p.35
16 Fiennes, (1983 edn.) p.265
17 Ward, 1700 (quoted by Cresswell 1985, p.39)
18 Rackham, 1983, p.53
19 Havinden, 1981, p.73
20 Moore, 1982, p.6
21 Aston, 1985, p.100
22 Aston, 1985, p.32
23 Cunliffe, 1971, pp.1 and 2
24 Havinden, 1981, p.129
25 Leland (ed. Toulmin-Smith 1910) Vol.V, p.166
26 Leland (ed. Toulmin-Smith 1910) Vol.I, p.139
27 Historical and Local New Bath Guide, 1802, p.118
28 Tunstall, 1889 edn., p.117
29 Collinson, 1791, p.145
30 Grigson, 1966, p.311
31 Collinson, 1791, p.145
32 Leland, (ed. Toulmin-Smith 1910) Vol.I, p.139
33 Collinson, 1791, p.151
34 Grigson, 1966, p.366
35 Jones, 1858
36 Britton, 1832, p.145
37 Chandler, 1735
38 Fiennes, (1983 edn.), p.40
39 Thomas, 1984, p.236
40 Pococke, 1754, (1889), Vol.I, p.153
41 Chandler, 1735
42 Ibbetson et al., 1793, p.143
43 Leland (ed. Toulmin-Smith 1910) Vol.V, p.98
44 Scott, 1984, p.5
45 King, 1895, p.25
46 Little, 1975, p.10
47 Pococke, 1754 (1889 edn.), p. 153
48 Universal Magazine, 1754
49 Chandler, 1735
50 Ison, 1980, p.126
51 Defoe, 1724-7 (1769 edn.), p.301
52 Pope, 1713, (quoted by Hunt and Willis, 1975, p.207)
53 Derrick letter, 10 May 1763 (quoted by Duke, 1984)
54 Chandler, 1735
55 Defoe, 1724-7 (1769 edn.), p.301
56 Pope, 1734, (quoted by Barrell, 1972, p.47)
57 Jones, 1858
58 Sitwell, 1945 (1960 edn.), p.221
59 Fielding, 1749 (1973 edn.), pp.58 and 545
60 Defoe, 1724-7 (1769 edn.)
61 Richardson, 1753 (quoted by Hunt and Willis, 1975, p.72)
62 Chandler, 1735
63 Universal Magazine, 1754
64 Pococke, 1754 (1889 edn.), Vol.II, p. 153
65 Stroud, 1975, pp. 214-247
66 Bath City Council Archives Ms.
67 Little, 1975, p.20
68 Stroud, 1975, p.230
69 Wittkower, 1974 (1983 edn.), p.178
70 Milton, 1667, Book IV, lines 445-451
71 Wood, 1765 (1969 edn.), p.352
72 Sydenham, 1907 (1969 edn.), p.11
73 Chandler, 1735
74 Evelyn, 1706 (1985 edn.), p. 154
75 Southey, 1807 (1984 edn.), p. 471
76 Wood, 1765 (1969 edn.), p.345
77 Wood, 1765 (1969 edn.), p.345
78 Ison, 1980, p.234
79 Mitchel, 1977, pp.100-102
80 Ison, 1980, p.234
81 Wood, 1765 (1969 edn.), p.320
82 Summerson, 1953 (1983 edn.), p.341
83 Ison, 1980, p.230

84   Summerson, 1953 (1983 edn.), p.101
85   Ison, 1980, p.239
86   Stroud, 1975, p.230
87   Ison, 1980, p.148
88   Watts, 1817, p.12
89   Ackerman, 1966, (1981 edn.), p.78
90   Pevsner, 1943 (1963 edn.), p.348
91   Southey, 1807 (1984 edn.), p.471
92   Ison, 1980, p.222
93   Neale, 1981, pp.231-238
94   Ison, 1980, p.222
95   Telford (quoted by Rolt, 1958 (1985 edn.), p.40)
96   Historical and Local New Bath Guide, 1802, p.104
97   Sydenham, 1907 (1969 edn.), pp.1 and 2
98   Sydenham, 1907 (1969 edn.), p.3
99   Sydenham, 1907 (1969 edn.), p.8
100  Sydenham, 1907 (1969 edn.), p.16
101  Sydenham, 1907 (1969 edn.), p.17
102  Sydenham, 1907 (1969 edn.), p.19
103  Sydenham, 1907 (1969 edn.), p.21
104  Historical and Local New Bath Guide, 1802, p.98
105  Summerson, 1980, p.70
106  Sydenham, 1907 (1969 edn.), p.25
107  Reynolds (quoted by Cook 1968 (1984 edn.), p.25)
108  Pevsner, 1943 (1963 edn.), p.356
109  Clark, 1928 (1962 edn.), p.3
110  Gilpin, 1768 (quoted by Hunt and Willis, 1975, p.337)
111  Clark, 1969 (1982 edn.), p.190
112  Humphreys, 1957 (1973 edn.), p.439
113  Payne Knight, 1805 (quoted by Cook, 1968 (1984 edn.), p.251)
     (see also Hunt and Willis, 1975, p.349)
114  Malins, 1966, p.45
115  Jones, 1858
116  Historical and Local New Bath Guide, 1802, p.101
117  Summerson, 1963, p.109
118  Ison, 1980, p.173
119  Pevsner, 1956 (1964 edn.), p.179
120  Ison, 1980, pp.16, 17, 175 and 180
121  Chalkin, 1974, pp.182, 183
122  Burke, 1756 (quoted by Temple, 1979, p.17)
123  Hogarth, 1753 (quoted by Eliot and Stern, 1979, p.71)
124  Pevsner, 1956 (1964 edn.), p.174
125  Pope, 1731 (quoted by Pevsner, 1956 (1964 edn.), p.174)
126  Ison, 1980, p.176
127  Neale, 1981, p.263
128  Historical and Local New Bath Guide, 1802, p.120
129  Page, 1911, Vol.II, p.341
130  Little, 1947, p.116
131  Southey, 1807 (1984 edn.), p.471
132  Summerson, 1953 (1983 edn.), p.485
133  Cook, 1968 (1984 edn.), p.268
134  Murray, 1963, p.139
135  Ackerman 1966, (1981 edn.), pp.53,54
136  Summerson, 1953 (1983 edn.), p.374
137  Summerson, 1953 (1983 edn.), p.532
138  Darley, 1975 (1978 edn.), p.84
139  Brown, 1982, p.78
140  Repton, 1816 (quoted by Grigson 1966, p.225)
141  Summerson, 1953 (1983 edn.), p.493
142  Repton (quoted by Darley, 1975, p.89)
143  Darley, 1975 (1978 edn.), p.63
144  Egan, 1819, p.35
145  Britton, 1832, p.162
146  Summerson, 1953 (1983 edn.), p.531
147  Wood, 1765 (1969 edn.), p.238
148  Chandler, 1735
149  Neale, 1981, p.228
150  Ison, 1980, p.14
151  Little, 1947, p.123
152  Loudon, 1833, p.1122
153  Cruikshank, 1985, p.95
154  Clark, 1928 (1962 edn.), p.3
155  Summerson, 1953 (1983 edn.), p.405
156  Clark, 1928 (1962 edn.), p.198
157  Warner, 1800, p.13
158  Payne Knight, 1808
159  Walpole (quoted by Pevsner, 1958, p.110)
160  Summerson, 1953 (1983 edn.), p.534
161  Granville, 1841, p.371
162  Summerson, 1953 (1983 edn.), p.532
163  Ison, 1980, p.189
164  Mitford, 1851, p.292
165  Black, 1888
166  Page, 1911, Vol.II, p.341
167  Neale, 1981, p.293
168  Neale, 1981, p.294
169  Taylor, 1973b, p.433
170  Olsen, 1976 (1979 edn.), p.209-211
171  Sedding (quoted by Carter, 1984, p.119)
172  Hadfield, 1960 (1985 edn.), p.258
173  Hadfield, 1960 (1985 edn.), p.303
174  Fleming and Gore, 1980, p.175
175  Fleming and Gore, 1980, p.186
176  Hadfield, 1960 (1985 edn.), pp.278-282
177  Bath Guide, 1832, p.lxvi
178  Bath Guide, 1832, p.lxiii
179  Bath Guide, 1851, p.58
180  Wheatcroft, 1897, p.30
181  Neale, 1981, p.259
182  Thomas, 1984, p.236
183  Curl, 1975, p.13
184  Penny, 1974, p.63
185  Tunstall, 1889 ed., p.107
186  Bath Guide, 1851, p.83
187  Bath Guide, 1851, p.127
188  Young, 1936 (1977 edn.), pp.41-46
189  Egan, 1819, p.268
190  Wheatcroft, 1897, p.43
191  Muthesius, 1982, p.247
192  Unwin, 1909 (1919 edn.), p.386
193  Unwin, 1909 (1919 edn.), p.294
194  Jackson, 1985, p.98
195  Unwin, 1909 (1919 edn.), pp.3 and 4
196  Edwards, 1981, p.107
197  Warner, 1800, p.3
198  Edwards, 1981, p.113
199  Abercrombie et al., 1930, p.92
200  Abercrombie et al., 1930, p.49
201  Abercrombie et al., 1930, p.139
202  Abercrombie et al., 1945, p.110
203  Abercrombie et al., 1945, p.98
204  Abercrombie et al., 1945, p.84
205  Abercrombie et al., 1945, p.81
206  Abercrombie et al., 1945, p.82
207  Chambers, 1791, (1825 edn., quoted by Eliot and Stern, 1979, p.33)
208  Summerson, 1953 (1983 edn.), p.391
209  Young, 1936 (1977 edn.), p.46
210  Barrell, 1972, pp.1 and 2
211  Clark, 1928 (1962 edn.), p.21
212  Pevsner, 1956 (1964 edn.), p.181
213  Pope, 1751 (quoted by Hunt and Willis, 1975, p.212)
214  Virgil, 1958 edn., Book VII, line 136
215  Pevsner, 1956 (1964 edn.), p.181

# Index